New Christian Poetry

Alwyn Marriage lectures in Philosophy and History of Art at the
University of Surrey, where she also teaches poetry and co-
ordinates the university's literature programme. She was for a
number of years poetry editor for *New Fire* before becoming poetry
editor and member of the editorial board of *Christian*. She writes
and lectures widely on spirituality, and her book on the Holy Spirit,
Life-Giving Spirit, was published by SPCK in 1989. She is married
with two daughters.

New Christian Poetry

Edited by Alwyn Marriage

Collins
FLAME

First published in Great Britain in 1990 under the
Flame imprint by the Religious Division of Collins
Publishers, 8 Grafton Street, London W1X 3LA

Copyright in each poem belongs to the individual
poet. Copyright in this collection, © 1990 Alwyn
Marriage

Text design by Malcolm Harvey Young

Printed and bound in Great Britain by William Collins
Sons & Co. Ltd, Glasgow

for Zoë

a much-loved Christian poet

Contents

Foreword

Christian truth and poetic expression are not strangers to each other, for to express our deepest thoughts we naturally use the most beautiful and powerful language of which we are capable. But devotional literature, however perceptive and inspiring, is not necessarily great poetry. The purpose of this anthology is to present, to Christian and non-Christian alike, poems which not only grow out of a genuine response to the Christian gospel, but which also deserve to take their place amongst the finest English poetry now being written.

In order to find the best new Christian poetry the net had to be cast as wide as possible. Publicity was therefore sent to members of the Poetry Society, to all clergy in Britain, to churches and magazines throughout the land, requesting that 'contemporary Christian poetry' be submitted for consideration.

The trouble with casting the net wide, however, is that one hauls in an enormous number of fish. In the months following our invitation for submissions, eight and a half thousand poems were received, from amongst which I was required to make a selection for an anthology of some two hundred pages. The poems came from all over the world: from established poets and those who had never published before; from people of all ages and educational backgrounds, of all denominations and none; and the quality was, naturally, extremely varied. The most clearly unsuitable were returned fairly promptly; but from then on the task became more and more difficult, as many poems which deserved to be included were eliminated, simply because of lack of space.

Many people have wondered what criteria were employed for selecting the best of contemporary Christian poetry. Not very surprisingly, the first, and most important, consideration was that it must be good *poetry*. What was being judged was not the quality of religious experience or insight, but the poem embodying that experience or insight. A number of poems moved me deeply at a personal level, several I would have no hesitation in recommending to someone seeking for Christ or struggling with darkness or doubt; but unless they had real merit as *poems* they found no place in this anthology.

Other poems were rejected because they were not truly *contemporary*. By inviting people to submit contemporary Christian poetry we hoped to indicate that we were looking for poetry that grows out of its own age, either by aligning itself with twentieth-century developments of form or by contributing something fresh to the tradition of an historical style. We do not need pastiche, for poetry survives through the ages and we have, in the English language, a veritable treasury of wonderful poetry from former ages. This can and should be savoured and enjoyed, without being imitated.

Victorian hymnody, for example, has had a deep and lasting effect on the poetic expression of religious experience, for it was the diet on which many Christians were nurtured. No modern renderings of Victorian hymn-style, however, appear in this anthology, for we have a rich enough store of such hymns already. The most praiseworthy examples of this particular genre will survive because they have an integrity which springs from their reflecting the reality of their own age. We are no longer in that age (even in the Church!), and those who write poetry are required to be explorers, pushing at the boundaries of language, developing styles that will better express the human condition as we now understand it. Poetry, like religion, is not static, and we are part of the forward march of poetry, contributing in our small ways to a response to T.S. Eliot's challenge that we should 'purify the dialect of the tribe'.

But to look for truly contemporary poetry is not limiting. Established forms from the past are not automatically to be rejected, for if sonnet form, or rhyming couplets, or the ballad, are allowed to live and grow, they can still be vehicles for fresh poetic expression. So those who expect all contemporary poetry to be in the form of blank verse will have a few surprises in store as they discover the wide variety of forms represented in this anthology.

Having said that it was primarily the poetry that was being judged, the qualifying 'Christian' was also an essential element in the selection. The poems in this book express different facets of what it means to be a Christian living, loving and praying in the world now. Christians are not protected from life but thrown into it to love Christ in the real world. The everyday concerns of ordinary people therefore become the stuff of religious expression, and this poetry reflects the infinite variety of ways in which people come to know God.

One of the tasks facing the Christian artist is to help others to see that all of life is sacred, is filled with God; and this principle is reflected in my choice of poems. Doubt and despair, honest reactions to the world and to other people, revelations that come to us through the natural world or through art, are all part of our contemporary religious experience and find a place in this anthology, even when they are not expressed in ostensibly religious terms.

In these poems there are some striking new images which leap out of the page to open our eyes to the wonder and glory of God. Once one has seen the crucified Christ as a wound in the sky, not only does twentieth-century art begin to make more sense, but the message of the incarnate God suffering and dying for love of human beings can shake us more forcefully. To meditate on the experience of watching for a kingfisher, with all the patience, unpredictability, yet assurance that our waiting will be rewarded, will help us to persevere in the adventure of prayer. To see God in the leaves dancing in the gutter, or in the face of an enemy, or the lonely tattered scarecrow in the field, will sharpen our awareness of the divine presence and teach us to open our eyes to see the eternal God embedded within this world, overflowing with self-giving love.

Without the fresh insights of poetry we risk becoming entrenched in well-worn, but sometimes outworn, images. 'Lamb of God', we chant wearily, untouched by the spine-tingling thrill with which early Christian converts living within an ancient Middle Eastern culture would have responded to this metaphor. The idea of sacrificing an animal, cutting its throat on the altar and letting it bleed to death, is simply not part of our experience, religious or otherwise. Lambs, for us, represent either the cuddly woolly toys of the nursery — which leads us to sentimentality — or the rather stupid creatures out on the hills, mindlessly following each other into danger or standing in the middle of the road to gape at our approaching car. Neither of these associations has much to offer as intense spiritual experience and it is no longer possible for us to get inside the minds and experience of those early worshippers, for whom the image of the Lamb of God would have set up intensely powerful reverberations.

In selecting these poems I was aware that tastes differ and that, although any anthology is bound to reflect the taste of the editor, personal preference should not be the only guiding principle. Anthologists, as well as the general reading public, are capable of recognizing merit in works which are not necessarily their own favourites, and to achieve balance in a work of this nature it is important to exercise this faculty. The wide variety in this collection should ensure that everyone will find something to enjoy and treasure, though the other side of that coin is that no one is likely to appreciate every one of the poems.

Most traditional anthologies of Christian poetry begin with the assumption that there is such a thing as a Christian poet, from amongst whose poetry one can choose representative works which are most obviously religious. In this anthology all the poems were chosen from the enormous pool received, irrespective of authorship; though, not surprisingly, works by several well-known poets were found to merit inclusion. The collection therefore took shape around the poems themselves, rather than around the poets.

This is why the anthology has a form which relates neither to the chronology or importance of individual poets, but to the theme and subject matter of the works themselves. The section on 'Times and Festivals', for instance, moves steadily through the Christian year, and in 'The Natural World' the poems have been grouped in a coherent order.

These poems reflect the reality of living as Christians in the world as it now is. It is therefore natural that they should include beauty and humour, anger and pain, vitality, insight, love and awe. Some can be used as prayers, some are oblique, others are thought-provoking; but all are, in their various ways, celebrating life, both human and divine. They are therefore offered in wonder and praise of God, whose glory and goodness we see in all around us, and through whom we enter into the fullness of life and love.

ALWYN MARRIAGE

The Natural World

Dear Saint Francis

Some creatures of our God and King
distract one at funeral moments
trundle across the floor on six legs
in their own gospel procession

Other creatures of our God and Queen
pop in and out feeding young
at the frantic nestbox when I try to join
in spirit in commital prayers.

DIANA DOWNING

Reflections

An old woman, sitting among petunias
Shelling broad beans,
Delivers one pale green baby after another:
Lumpy forehead, tucked-up legs,
Green placenta below.
She thinks of rice grains, pouring from the jar,
And blow-flies' eggs on meat;
She thinks of water at the plug-hole,
The swirling hearts of daisies,
And far imagined nebulae;
And of herself, a tiny creator
Delighting in all she makes.
An old woman, sitting in the sunshine,
Ponders on the economy of God.

STEPHANIE GIFFORD

Beachcomber

Come beachcomber Spirit
search the shores
of my life;
bring to remembrance
Love's presence.

GILLIAN MARY, SSC

Two Nature Poems

Here,
beneath the azure sky
I find you.

Lost
in your immensity,
with a cool wind
fanning my cheek

and the grass
June sweet.

Looking out
over rolling Somerset
fields
in the glazed heat,

or sitting
in the hush of evening
feasting
on blood-red paeonies,

Your softness creeps upon us,
unaware,
in the silences that hang
on the still air.

Lord
I glimpse you

like a young deer,
flitting between streams.

A gleam of flank,
or antler:

a hoof thud
on turf.

Too swift for me,
your leaps.

Too delicate
your poise.

KATHERINE CHARNLEY

August in the Quantocks

1. The eye of the lizard
   Holds the gold on the green
   We are still, as one,
   And the sun heals.

   Only the brown hum of bees
   Reaches my listening.

2. The hills sleep
   In the mauve of my seeing
   The sky's slow calm
   Flows
   Through the lungs of my soul
   Breathing out and breathing in
   Deeper now, deeper
   Than end of summer lavender,

   And the long dark's sighing
   Fans the membrane of my being.

BRIDGET JOSEPH

Wood Work

There is spent rain
clinging to a tree —
intermittently a drop catches colour —
the branches spread
to a different purpose
from the ordinary

Each globe waterscaped
independently — unmelting
a tremorless brilliancy —
shed rain makes wetly
beautiful a bare tree
branch rungs
of radiant energy
Jacob's ladder
placed for me.

CAROLINE ACKROYD

Autumn's Passion

Now rapidly fall, as I walk, the leaves;
   Brown and yellow, they tumble, scatter and skim;
   Breeze brushes them, boot rustles them; dim
Fragment of damp to the windy pavement cleaves;
     The trees grow slim.

Sweeper, armed with barrow and broom, arrives;
   Brown and yellow are scraped with it, bunched within
   Four metal walls for their journey to heap or bin;
Lost are the whispering shapes; no sap survives;
     Decay sets in.

Leaves, where are you soon when winter raves?
   Brown and yellow depart stark twigs; worms clean
   Lawns for a meal of foliage; dead the green.
But down in the death is the mould the microbe saves,
     All eyes unseen;

Loam, leaf-fruit, feeder of roots, then weaves,
   Brown and rich, the beds where seeds may dream
   Till, spring-cracked, they with the lengthening beam
Of sun, arise. Slowly the soil conceives.
     The new shoots gleam.

Tree, stripped of its bark, its twigs, its leaves,
   Brown and stark, on Golgotha hill is seen,
   A dead man's limbs for branches; where life has been
Winter on wood now reigns; but for one who believes
     Easter springs green.

HENRY MAYOR

West

Hand over eyes as the road bends
Into the level sun I see
The sign at the roundabout: West.

And wherever I'm heading, west
Draws the unfocused mind. The world,
The day, roll steadily that way.

There's a sea in the sky. All round,
A tide floats land-locked hills, blue backs
Blunt heads gathering to swim west.

Men digging in gardens straighten
Their backs, turn west to watch the flood
Brimming and gleaming behind trees.

In valley towns aground in shade
A ripple on a wall, a blaze
Of estuary over roofs

And in the gaps of houses call
People to their doors, gazing west.
There's something in the way. West is

An old ache for the land's end, nothing
Between, for the clean arc of sea
And sky, the pure circle of sun

And the sun's momentum over
The rim and edge of things, not now,
But coming, when the night draws in.

MARGARET COOKE

Three Haiku: Taizé

the hills are furred
with gentleness,
sing soft songs
of everlasting joy.

white thistledown floats high
spiralling trustingly
into a blue sky.

slowly the corn ripens,
warmth fills my heart;
all is growing towards God.

ALWYN MARRIAGE

After Injury

Some miracles are slow:
white lilac each returning Spring
(whiter than all detergent claims);
healing of tissue — failing that,
the spirit's adaptation, achievement of serenity;
faith's slow gestation — many months or years,
a lifetime even;
(and who can know how long a labyrinth of thought
the Spirit threaded
that Paul should see a sudden light?);
awareness of Your presence
— though always there.

How many miracles in soul or body
go without recognition?
the nerve that grows, the strengthened will,
better relationships,
developing compassion.

Some miracles don't happen, but
miraculously
there are alternatives.

WINIFRED YOUNG

Old Age

The maples are burning,
Kindled with a silent flame,
Like russet torches in the forest depths.
I hear no splutter or crackle of resin,
Yet they burn and burn.

Does He see them,
Offering this last sacrifice of summer?
Does He see them in a different time,
Flower in fire,
And suddenly put on winter?

For us, in exquisite slowness,
They turn in the cool embrace of Autumn.
In silent dance,
The leaves curl, blush, flame out,
In appalling submission,
To bring him this yearly gift of colour,
amid the Autumn drab.

Lord, in my old age grant me
One last passionate flowering —
Let love burn off my summer green,
In sudden, splendid fire.

TIM MARKS

Taproot

Branches and boughs
Bow and brittle — break —
In December winds.
Grey with death they stand
Stiff into the chilling air.
Still the heart plods on.

Deep in steel the taproot thrusts,
hurts and grips tight.

In the softer time
the tree will grow great
with green. And life will crowd.
Still the heart plods on.

Deep in the earth the taproot
Thrusts and clings
and holds fast.

PENNY SIDES

Ferry Meadows

A view from the verandah:
I can see a windsurfer's sail
magenta, yellow, blue, tactfully glide
along the wrinkling water's surface.
I can see how one cannot view
the conundrum of existence
save in its kaleidoscope quirkdom;
the fishes, the air-breathers,
the air-winging evening hordes,
noisily together telling me something,
something hitherto unworded,
and still remaining wordless.

M.P. GREEN

As a lichee nut

Shrivels to release
Its sweet
So my skin will fall
Away to a still small
Beat of heart
Hidden in the hurt
Where past and present
Meet and part.

SARA LEE STADELMAN

The Uncertainty of Love

I didn't quite see the cormorant
Out on the wind-blown waves
Only the waves.
The point of the joke I missed
In the company of friends
Only the ends of smiles were left.
I was looking at the sunlight on the grass
When the idea was launched
And only guessed at its significance.

When others found that they were in the swim
I stood by the empty swimming pool.
Your eyes tell me much, but
At translation from one language to another
I was never much good.
I am at risk. And mistranslations
Are the difference between
Grey melancholy and the stars.

JOHN COPUS

Kingfisher

If Christ our king could
In the ammoniac stench of the stable
Suffer at His nativity to be
Neighbour to slow-breathing beasts,

Then small wonder that the kingfisher's
spark should be struck
In a damp underworld of willow root and worm
Where vole and water rat splash,

For once the shells split and sapphire
And fire opal fledge in their filth
And six or seven small spurts of flame
Are tumbled out into the dazzle,

Then earth, air, fire and water meet
In a perfection of balance, trafficking,
Like prayer, between this world and that.
And isn't it then that their mother's

Fabled and other self is said to brood
On a nest of bones, calming the waters,
And granting us glimpses of Eden
In those Mary-blue halcyon days?

NEIL CURRY

Song of the Shearwater, based on Psalm 139

O Lord you have searched out
    my flight path
    over the oceans.

        Even before my cry
        filled the night
        with thousands of
        others
        homing in to burrows
        on Ynys Enlli
        you knew my journey.

You guided my parents
    in late February
    to this place,
    protected them
    as each sat in turn
    on one white egg.

        For fifty Pentecostal days
        the great Bird of the Spirit
        hovering
        watched for the first
        signs of birth
        as the shell cracked.

Wonderful are your works:
    when I was being made
    in secret
    intricately wrought
    in the depths of the earth
your eyes beheld my unformed substance.

        You watched over
        the feeding flights
        of my parents
        sometimes over hundreds of miles

You guided them
    in the darkest hours
    of the night
    to the home burrow.

And then suddenly
my parents
deserted me
and for seven long days
I sat in the burrow
alone
too well fed
to get out!

If I make my bed in Sheol
watching and fasting
you are there also.

When the time came
I struggled out
onto the wall
above my burrow
to try my wings.

If I say let only darkness
cover me
it is because in your wisdom
you made me ungainly
on land

but when I take
the wings of the morning
before dawn
I fly
with easy grace
over the oceans.

I praise you:
wonderful are your works.
Guide me in the everlasting
Way.

GILLIAN MARY, SSC

Lauds

The congregation of the birds at dawn
With unoiled throats screech each one louder than the next
In protest at the neighbour who disturbs his peace;
Whilst always there is one who kneels apart
For bathing in the silent dews of love.

DOUG CONSTABLE

Testudo

1. Embedded diamonds spell the girl's name.
    A living casket — it skids
    on the polish and is put back to GO.

    'What will you do when it is dead?'
    asked Mr Samgrass. 'Can you have
    another tortoise fitted to the shell?'

    Don't laugh: these things happen.
    But I wonder if my pain, grafted
    to another's, will shrivel or swell?

2. The story has it, that all ships
    go more slowly when carrying
    the right foot of a tortoise on board.

    So when the wind dropped
    and the lumbering stowaway was found
    below deck, your course was clear.

    But you were worried, not knowing
    your right from your left,
    so you chopped off the other two too.

3. 'Why, boy, are you stroking the tortoise?
    To please it? Child! You might as well stroke
    the dome of St Paul's to please the Dean!'

    My vague, naïve beliefs hold firm.
    The body houses the spirit and the church
    is the house of God. My sluggish schooling

    shuns your elegant wit, and a word —
    latin of all things — is reassembling
    in my brain. *Religio:* I connect.

PAUL MUNDEN

Father Mole

You could move your mind to make a mountain
Out of the shy convictions you've bespoke,
You could unearth presumption, at a stroke
Evacuate its forthright, feral fountain,
Too deep almost for canons to restrain
Dig down into the darknesses that choke
The proud beneath their own demotic yoke,
Then out with reverend diffidence again.

Your bright words stress an hieratic ethos,
Insistent sibilants that soothe the soul,
Answers that compensate the sense of loss.

Your certain notions take us as we grope
Our lowly way along. You give us hope
Because you see what God is, Father Mole.

M.J. FOLEY

Least of Anything

A grain of sand
Upon the beach,
Warmed by the sun,
Washed by the sea,
Outside numeric reach.
Unnamed, unnumbered,
Closely nestling with its kind.
Undisturbed until the wind
Blows some dark
Pollution from the land,
That twists its very
Nature round,
And storms
Its tiny citadel
The centuries had bound.

VERA BOYLE

Maid and Mog

We grey together, my cat and I,
each with the thin glinting betrayal
of a few blond and silvery hairs
amidst the paint-black and red-tinged strands.
He and I both sleep most of the day,
somnolent as hibernating bears,
and then wake to eat, wash, defecate,
only to pass the night in twitching.
Sometimes with an unusual ease
we activate weary, ageing limbs
and sally forth into the harsh day —
he to chase birds, which are never caught,
me to catch men, who will never stay.
We sleep longer as life gets shorter,
senses turning inwards to our dreams
and we fade, making our life slower,
blending together with the last years.

POLLY BIRD

Prayer of the Franciscan's Cat

Lord,
it has been a bounteous summer,
Hop gardens in heat haze shimmered
though the voles were thin —
all sinners. Larks above the oast,
Old Reynard found dead by the bilberried ledge.
Now October,
still the last apples cling,
the walnut's coat spewn.
The earth renewed before winter's trumpet shrills.

So many pilgrims came
to where once was Blean Wood
visiting our hospital of St Nicholas.
I have sat on the kitchen step
resisting temptation.
One worrisome wasp have I eaten,
he went last to his hole,
now never to come first,
but letting loose inside me such a thirst
that I drank at the brook.

Lord,
the gentle Franciscans talk of Paradise
but for me it is here, with them
in our beloved church.

MARGARET BROWNE

Metamorphosis

caterpillar tracks
upon newly perforated leaf patterns
the tarpaulin of skin
pulled in
a slow, centripetal movement
of life,
which becomes
slower
and slower
and stabilizes
as the host dissolves
into its chrysalis
and as a butterfly
crystallizes
from its elixir.

IAN TODD

Eel-like

I twist
     and writhe
          eel-like
to escape the demands
          of an all-demanding Christ
               who asks more than I can bear.

I slip
     through a hole
          in the net
only to find he has put his hands underneath
          and I fall into them panting
               and very gradually relax.
It takes a long time to learn
          that you can't live a Christ-like life
            without Christ.

JOCELYN BAILEY

Farm

O God Thee I would worship though my arms
Unequal to the heavy land, and ploughshare rusted.
Into Thy fields return today that the slothful have neglected,
But shall not further derelict stand.

In Thy walled garden on the southern wall
   Thy vines and peaches set;
   Thy hay bring in to barn
   In a sweet June cut
(Never a thistle in Thy ryegrass and Thy clover)
Thy heifers before sunrise springing with new milk —
These would I walk to calves unto Thy shippon cool.

O working God Who sang Thy morning songs for joy
And singest ever new with such sweet shout,
Loosen our twisted chords, reset our bones,
And clarify and magnify our hearts O God.

   The labourers stand.
   Bind up our broken farms.
   Sharpen what steel Thou wilt.   DENIS KNIGHT

Fish

Under the waterfall of your love
I am like a frightened fish,
trusting, but unsure,
knowing only the transforming power
of the torrent.

In the shallows by the riverbank,
I feel more certain,
and prepare to join the direction
of the current.

At last I find
that I can float in it,
enjoying the swirl of the foam
in the rapids,
and the freshness of the froth
on the leading edge
of the waves.

Morning

The slushy-footed cow
swishing flies from its back
makes a murmuring moo
and lurches in the slurry
to the gate and the cursing cowman.

Smoke-shadows shift
from the heaving hill-back
and square-walled fields
are dew-steamy green
in the sun's yellow wake-up warmth.

Whirling swifts
carve slits in the air
as the farmer in the weather-washed
flint-grey milk-sheds
works with a clatter in the bucket.

BILL HOOPER

I will laugh at myself
till the cows come home,
and then I will pour the milk
of the ruminant fields
into my homeward pail.

KATHLEEN HERBERT
First published in *Tails and Tail Ends*

Hymn at Groundlevel

Under the windows, lizards with shaky throats the
colour of estuaries bowed like suave sages pondering the psalms,
    And ant-lions drew their spiralling scrolls down into the
conscious grains of the sand with the sleek gestures of votaries,
    All afternoon the orb-web weavers fasted in the snares of
Paradise and praised the shade,
    Dung-beetles trundled the sweet sticky muck of sacrifice
over an unloved soil
    While I comforted my eyes and mouth in the cold yellowy splash
of alamandas and studied attentiveness in their calm stems,
    The grasshopper in his Joseph's coat felt how he harmonized
with all the accents of the grateful leaves, and I could taste
    His ecstasy as he shone in the light.
    At nightfall, in the boarded tower, barn owls brought mice
to their clumsy children and reflected a bony moon in their petal
        faces;
    The inconspicuous gathering of yesterday's rain in a single
plump drop at the leaf's edge contained all significance;
    And at morning, the velvety antiphons of moths.

ERIC ORMSBY

Sanctuary

Just deep enough into my topmost leaves
that the sun can only side-slip into me
— my cathedral of green light,
birds gliding through my arches and cool cloisters
return each year, their children following.

Winds have not bent or humbled us,
we've simply spread ourselves along their flow.
We comfort each other through our roots,
and in the spring flap leaves to send slow messages,
mirage-patterns through the air:
young, I was thrilled by the aspen in the valley,
now it is the rowan I wait for.

We nurture our leaf-children all their lives
— how they cling to us before they spin away.

The sun feeds me from a violet spoon,
but vines remind me one day I shall fall,
sink into forest earth we churn each day; and are.
The leaves may soften in my knot-holes,
seedlings feed on me, grow tall.

The snow is melting. Soon the crane will come,
his hundredth time. I stretch inside my bark.

JOHN LATHAM

After the British Association Lecture

'Stardust,' he said. 'We're made
Of stardust,' and his eyes shone.
He surveyed the dark millennia,
Considering how the explosion
Rang and rippled with no walls
To hold it, studding the emptiness
With revolving sequins, and how,
On one pinhead, atom clunched
Upon atom, until the same current
Sparked man into the garden
To encounter his cousins, beasts,
Tree, fruit, snake, all built
From the same blocks, the same
Rubbings from the stars. And
Then came civilization.

Apeman Smith smiles at his victim.
Stardust, you said? And the napalm
Rattles in his pocket.

Yet search
And probe, deep under the coarsened
Lineaments. Is it possible
That behind that filthy glass
A shy candle still
Shudders? Does the eternal
Light survive unquenched
Humanity's dousing?

                    Or
Was the explosion, more dust
Than star, never the vehicle
Of spirit?

JEAN HARRISON

Honesty

Purple honesty
grows shadowed by lies as white
as apple blossom.

When the truth is dead, its seeds
will fall black upon the earth.

JEREMY YOUNG

Amen

Splashing of spangled tumbling waters
that drop, slide, and, spurting, fall and splinter;
the boisterous, rumbusting surfscudding, spray-cresting
surge of the clamorous thrash of the stream
to join the breaking of drifted and moon-swollen tides
on the long-forming, shore-changing pillow of
    rock-clothed and sandbedded face of earth
    is like
    the torrent of Pentecost
    spending all
to voice through the silence of nature's busy utterings,
the 'Amen' of God's children.

DOUG CONSTABLE

Place

The Kilns   To C.S. Lewis

A rambling house where academic talk
once buzzed and your pen stung Screwtape
and honey flowed when a foreign tongue,
witty with your faith, unsealed a bliss
deeper than logic. The odd bond sweetened,
breathed Grecian air, then found Greek tragedy,
fate's waspish venom. Joy limped up these stairs
and a final anguish shook the walls
free from legends of a dry scholar.

I feel the scorching irony
in this quiet room as I stroke the hollow
your shifting bulk wore in a big arm-chair.
The house-name prods faint images
of my Cornish youth: hot kiln-steam, bubbling clay,
thick suffocating powder-muffled rails
where a tank-waggon vomited. It's a way
of refining: some such jargon
I recall dimly. Not a trace
of its truth in my wedded life: I salute
your faith's hard test, but I am past my furnace.

I admire the autumn garden
which you blessed with her in timeless moments,
the bees around the flowers, hurting no-one;
and you went indoors to a feast, a foretaste,
the wine among spilled books by firelight,
your dream-tracks reaching unflawed planets,
your fancies solid in her puckish creed.

Here were the springs that fed me,
parched for hope amid sullen kilns;
and the present bounty, my wife's hand
guiding me to your door,
assures me that your blithe wisdom
rides now unwounded: Joy still hunts
for surprises, teasing after the grave sting.

JACK CLEMO

Lee Bay at Evening

Rock and tree blur in the mist's soft caress,
as the dove grey velvet cliff nudges the sea.

The sea shushes —
but its sibilant plea fills the silence.
The sun shines
and heaving lead is
hammered into beaten silver,
an honest alchemy.

Seagulls float,
beckoning speech marks,
waiting to be filled with my response.

Words teem,
tripping over themselves
in a frenzied attempt to be adequate.

But I say nothing —
and the sea goes on sighing,
disappointed but not surprised.

CHRISTOPHER ELLIS

Edmund, Martyr

St Edmund pray for . . .

> *pray for . . .*

>> *pray for . . .*

Subscribed, his feet —
a broken predicate; lips' patent
patient in repetition.

Yet Edmund here has gone beyond
the pain, the ecstasy,
who feels his griefs
as one once known
in the world
but who journeys on.

Shin, loin, breast, arm . . .
the little lurid stigmata
bright with their spurted blood-trefoils.
In painted light they hurt·
like jewels, gilt wounds —
the short, bright, gilded arrows.

His face: a mask. Plain —
from a plain century;
each curl of his blond saint hair
scrolled on his forehead.
A countenance of storm-calm,
of one who will not be touched more.

He is growing now from his gold-leaf oak
to his seat in the company
that may intercede, that may speak for us
in our withering lives
in our cramp of earth; in our need

in our great need.

STUART HENSON
(from *Figures from a Norfolk Church*)

East Anglian Meditation

All the same these seeming, sense of chill churches,
glory of men's making for a better maker.
They built best here, burdening angels with
the vast roofspan, intricately carving wood
lit with gold saints and Saxon kings.

Out here we rest beside the river where
masons have not cut stone, nor craftsmen
of stained glass made blue and scarlet panes
to decorate the Anglian light. Here gathering
of reeds is the grebe's glory, now and forever,
and heron's flight is a leap to paradise.

ANGELA RIGBY

Jesus Revisits
St Just-in-Roseland

I came here in my youth. It was
Almost too long ago
For remembering. Truth is lost
Under the snow
Of the centuries; though the tides now,
As then, beckon, and the heron
Flies languorously. Plough-
Shares may turn up flints, and rain

Expose old artefacts, but
The tin has gone that Joseph
Of Arimathea sought.
Spume has given way enough
For us to berth along this creek;
It was evening when we came ashore,
Glad, but nearly too tired to speak.
We slept in a warm hut, the roar

Of the sea hushed to the regular breathing
Of those present. Our cargo loaded,
We left the very next evening
— Though not before I had climbed, and stood,
Looking upon this peaceful scene.
The traders called. I scampered down;
And we set off with the setting sun
Towards that far, familiar town

In the Levant where Mary went
About her business. In two months' time
We would recall the hours we spent
. In this cool land. The sublime
Autumn would quicken into winter;
Snow might fall, though we would see
None of it. My father would enter,
Carrying wood for carpentry;

Noises in the street would diminish
Memory; but in my dreams
I sailed back here, as if to finish
Unfinished business. The caulked seams,
The taut sails, the song of the crew:
Everything conspired towards
Renewing what only dreams can renew
Within a landscape beyond words.

PAUL GROVES

Recently I've been Thinking of Blue

Recently I've been thinking of blue
the blue of the mosque in Istanbul
and the Pudding Shop where we signed our names
looking for notes from people we knew who'd been there before.
That night we split from the rest and headed north again
hitching through rain
and the fine line between boredom and despair
till we got to Prague — the flat you borrowed from a friend
(you said you didn't know then it was only one room).

I've been thinking of blue — the river — the Danube?
pierced by the spire of St Vitus Cathedral —
all the cathedrals in Europe that year and this is the one I
remember by name:
the symmetry perfectly scaled to inflame.
And I thought if there is a God, he is here
in this city with so many churches, and you a Jew.
Then you disappeared
into the winding streets of a language you didn't even speak
looking for condoms . . . I grinned to myself
and counted one more hurdle (almost) cleared
in the obstacle course to maturity,
until you returned with two ice creams
'It's all I could find I'm afraid',
so I learned about abstinence too.

Recently I've been thinking of blue,
of your eyes when we put our foreheads together —
if there were a God
I suppose he would have impossibly blue eyes too;
some days I long to climb inside
and rest along the crest of those lids
rocked while the waves of your breathing
slowly cover me over
till nothing remains
but the memory of you and that summer in Prague.

KATIE CAMPBELL
First published in *Prospice*

House of the Holy

I
stand
alone and
watch the sun
shine through the
stained-glass windows
in an explosion of colour.
The altar bathed in light
returns God's holiness
through its cross
upon which my
eyes rest
while
a
musty
fragrance
fills my mind
and takes me away
to a new-found Utopia.
I honour it but perhaps I
am to feel sorrow or will
I experience feelings
of pain if ever I
am to go away
from this
place
I
am in?
Slowly an
urge fills me
and I want to cry
aloud and pray to God.
This magnificent monument
has lasted since earliest
times and will always
belong to my soul.
Oh peoples of
old shall
never
a
more elegant sight behold.

ANDREW STICKLAND

Crossing the Severn

Coming out of England's broader weave,
The bridge threads me.
My cotton yarn,
Unravelled by the prying year-fingers,
Trails behind its slender course,
Longing for pattern
And the Craftsman's steady eye
To reassert His will.

The grubby, woollen hills
Are closely knit with silver streams.
Long needles gouged them,
Drawn to the sea
Across a damp and pliant coat.

Houses barely hold their grey.
Brighter shades would long have run
And spoilt the stone with pastel dyes,
More fitting to an island sun.

But here,
Here there are no stains.
Nor stitch, fallen like an angel.

Secure through the towering eye
I set on land
And feel again the Weaver's gentle hands
At work upon my cloth.

NIGEL PRICE

Dewi Sant

Prayer with the fortitude
                    of bracken and the streaming tide
has weathered men and shouldered
                    all history aside
and stands still, cloud and fire,
                    a pillar by day and night.
Stanch, silence, that sharp trickle
                    of words to the mind.

Enough now to let the sea
                    blow through, to sip the wind
again as layers of sky
                    clear where the hills stand.
Shiftless as flesh and blood
                    in the age of the saints,
these men blew and were blown,
                    seeds finding no place
for haven, but still laying
                    eleven hundred years of peace.
That long ago Euclid
                    served as plumb-line and level
to the men of trades who hoisted
                    each new cathedral
out of the sky, and as long
                    had served clerkish pupils
as rubric hovering by
                    while Punic and Gallic wars
scooped the Roman bowl,
                    the homeland of laws.
But squirrelling succulents
                    underfoot owned no cause.
On shoreline and cliff
                    hymns echoed in the caves —
unison or wind-gnawing choughs,
                    blotched Welsh stone, cold waves.
David, Columba, Non
                    and Patrick nourished these airs,
heather, the river reddening
                    crabs in their jetty lairs.
Now they themselves are present;
                    their silence instils the days.
Pillars of the invisible
                    landscape tremble with praise.

MARTIN TURNER

The Olde Priory

Remember the convent?
It's a restaurant now.
The few remaining nuns
renamed themselves
and left for a bungalow on the hill.
The imprint of time lingers
in the small windows,
the stone walls
that restrain table talk to whispers.

I sat opposite Anne,
a candle-light between us,
was bemused by the menu
wondering how a monkfish
entered a nuns' priory
and felt good when I ate him
knowing he was an intruder
in a place of holies,
where nuns bent over pews,
fasting, abstaining,
meditating on the passion
for a smidgen of peace.

Now, the new faithful congregate
around the cloister tables
avoiding thoughts of heaven
for fear of altitude sickness
that might reduce
their gastronomic pleasures.
They thirst and hunger,
the chef is guru,
the coy waitresses, Angels.

The Olde Priory is comfortable
with time:
It fed the soul
it feeds the body.
As you leave
the door latch click-clanks
old time — new time.

NOEL MONAHAN

St John and St Anselm

Grinning derisively from the twin towers
of the Church of St John and St Anselm
the gargoyles mockingly survey
the empty cans, the paper and discarded cartons,
the battered headstones and neglected graves.

A few years ago St John
and St Anselm, like the nearby
Mount of Olives, still remained a church.
Now it is used by the youthful unemployed
who take part in activities arranged
by Arts Opportunities Limited,
while the Mount of Olives is a Fitness Centre,
where unconcerned with spiritual longing
the faithful seek only the health of the body.

Doubtless St John, a shadowy mystic,
should he ever come this far north,
would gaze sadly at 'our beloved father'
beneath a broken cross, at 'dear mother'
pathetically askew in the long grass.
Yet absorbed by ineffable divinity,
having long ago witnessed the light
shining in the uncomprehending darkness,
he might be consoled that the building
is put to a seemingly useful purpose.
Quietly departing he might murmur:
'I have seen this happen before.
Soon there will be a new beginning.'

But surely Anselm, stubborn Norman saint,
reluctant archbishop to an evil king,
would react in a manner less quiescent.
Loving the English as he loved his Church,
having spent much of his life struggling
successfully against the power of the State,
he would turn away in obvious anguish.
Then oblivious of the traffic he would go
striding instinctively towards the Cathedral,
shouting angrily through his tears:
'My people, has it come to this?
Have you forgotten who you are?
Do you no longer care?'

RAYMOND TONG
First published in *Encounter*

Halfway to Assisi

A trattoria near Orvieto,
Sun trying to transcend the Abruzzi,
Three bees were drawn toward the wine of our love;
I took their stingers willingly in hand
To save the milk of your neck from spoiling;
You tossed long years of hair indifferently,
Used to having others suffer for you;
I was halfway to the saint called Francis,
Intent on leaving you to weep away;
You were half again away from his Clare,
The antithesis of poverty frieze;
But when we arrived you stayed inside walls,
And I had to look for a rich Lady.

THOMAS KRETZ

Visiting Josephine Butler's Grave
at Kirknewton Churchyard

Screech of peacock
across a still day

On the road verge
peacock feathers
tasselled ribs
collected
for a brighter memento

Celandine in the stream

Birdsong Bee Drone

Lichen on the gravestone

Fingers tracing
time-blurred letters
in warm stone
such strong passion
drowned in grief
and transformed.

GEOFFREY SMITH

Eisten

Outside the chapel at Eisten
Three prams were parked.
We hesitated.

On separate pews
Three girls
Each guiding her doll's arm

To make the sign of the cross.
Shyly they rose to genuflect
And hurry out

Leaving us in the dim light
Too awkward
To cross ourselves.

LYDIA HARRIS

Carthusian Monastery: Capri

Oleanders, their leaves shed
like so many years.
A bud like the tip of the bloody spear
that wounded Christ.
A well with a broken rope, swinging
gently, so, so . . .
and somewhere above the courtyard
a singing halo of bees, part
of an invisible flowering chestnut;
some tree of heaven, anyway.

GEOFFREY HOLLOWAY

Adam in Northumberland

Eden was not an olive grove, it was not
the sun-caked, lavender-pungent hillside,

but carapace of copper, emerald and gold,
cleansed by the flowing caustic
of aseptic indigo skies.

How long men have played on this garden,
and been ordered inside, leaving behind
their cups — willow-pattern, Samian —
and those ring-stains on the rocks;

hanging their heads, knowing they,
like us, had broken their promises.

FIONA HALL

The Sky's Badge

A long way from love and nowhere to go,
In a desert of dreams where cactus stand,
Insects ride on the swollen rock, slow
Snakes fawn on the sun.

Water is love and air is life. The sand
Blossoms with skeletons of pain.

Farther than all the others, there is one,
Four-ways fast on a hill, and the sky's badge.
Beneath this sign, I do not thirst in vain,
Though lush oases dim the dry mirage.

JAMES RUSSELL GRANT
from *The Excitement of Being Sam*

Deflections in Early Summer

A stained-glass window with Gothic arch
embellishes the eastern wall above the altar.
Tripartite and pedestrian in its art
the window depicts excerpts from the Bible:
stylized, innocuous, symbolic, bland,
classically chaste, formally balanced,
pinioned with lead.

Sometimes as I stand, hymn-book in hand,
My eyes searching haphazardly about the church,
(as if faith might be found behind a pillar),
sunlight pours headlong through the glass
undoing the craftsman's deft precision
and stippling the plain cream northern wall,
that flanks the chancel beside the organ pipes,
with muted rainbow patchwork, fluid fantasy;
wild medley of bubbling globules, mish-mash
of floating figments trellised in mottled magic:
lavishing uninhibited delight on the bare plaster,
spilling immoderate joy on the bare surface
of my soul.

All symmetry is gone; the gospel is confounded.
Yet that mystic message of light-hearted hope,
spelled out by the science of refraction,
speaks to me more volubly than all
the scriptures can.

BETTY SHEPHERD

Teachers and Tourists

he spoke so fast (as he addressed us from the platform)
we drowned under a hail of words

slides were shown (back to front)
of onion-shaped mosque temples
huge towers lancing spears of hate for salman rushdie's
secret hide-out

do buddhas still contemplate by the girders of ficus
religiosa? fig trees assemble their geometric structure

what will be will determine how we see
our own humanity

this was a missionary report
workers are sent in the guise of tourists
living out of a smuggled suitcase

as if we were the ones with hand-out answers
as if our jaded culture had made us wiser
are you a filipino?
for you, the cock could crow three times

you might find the body of your brother shot by
revenge squads
a western hand on an eastern throat
is this dialogue?

teachers and tourists
blind guides
trapped in the ditch of orthodoxy

ALEX WARNER

The Olive Trees

The olive trees still breathe in Gatch Manu,*
even those that saw the waving of palms,
even those that felt the traitor's kiss.
Locked within their roots, they give back nothing.

Was this a myth that led us to the Hill,
searching for some sunday school certainties?
Rejected by the ancient bone-gatherers
whose harvest awaits another time.
Was it arrogance which led us to assume
that half-denying we could wait for cock crow
or half-believing we could take this bread?

DEREK K. DURBRIDGE

*Hebrew for Gethsemane

The Dowry of Mary

The autumn rose hangs rusting
From a brittle gibbet of thorn.
In this garden the ancient church
Waits behind its empty gates. Pause;
Within is stillness, intense with decay,
Sweet as shrouds. Through a hazed lancet
The sun coin sinks through seawater.
The air aches for the flowers withered here,
For candles sighed out at shrines now dismantled —
Lampless cancelled saint-effaced sanctuaries.
The pews strain as breakwaters against
The slow erosion of encroaching oceans,
Unsouling stretches of wasting sea
That yearn on desolate distances of shore.
The sands at the door are cool to the feet;
In the aisles the sand is damp. Drifted dunes
Shift where the eastern cliffs rise sheer.
The white seabird still visits here, touching
Briefly, a few, with quiet wings,
Where once it soared haloed, and flew
From skilful hands, such as raised churches,
Upon the heads of uncounted people,
Whispering waves on a wide beach.
These were the generations who saw God
Walk with child's feet on their grass
And saw his circled face in a bright cup.
They called their church-proud acres
England, the Dowry of Mary, whose roses
Garlanded unendingly. Now
A few petals float home on evening tides.
The drowned dead are still earthed.
And sometimes too a bell
Recalls to us submerged rocks and reefs;
And an echo of incense breathes myrrhy
Of the secret whiteness in the heart of the stones
Which close these English garden-tombs.

R. HUGHES

People

We Hug with Words

This is letter-writing night,
if you look up to my window
you'll see nothing but curtained light.

The radiator is warm in here,
my old black Remington sings
and I'm drunk on vintage good-cheer.

Friends parted by sea and land,
their roots dug deep in my life:
we hug with words, not arms and hands.

The thrill of unfamiliar post-marks
on foreign stamps found:
I enter, open-armed, this ark.

For twenty of my thirty years
I've penned letters, most sang
at least one (if not three) cheers —

about a shared past — a holy glow
all mixed up with the domestic:
'Liz is washing dinner dishes below,

after I cooked vegetable crumble . . .'
Bravo for such utter humdrum.
It makes life tick and keeps me humble.

LOUIS HEMMINGS

Breathing

Breathing does not come naturally.
The baby is slapped into it.
The old ride it like a horse
that shies and rears and finally bolts —
so there is no catching up with it.

Children spend breath like water
Not caring how hard to come by it is for the old.
They bowl it in hoops of sound in alleys,
kick cans of it along pavements.

They are always laughing with it
as if it grew on trees, as if it could be
plucked from the air in great gulps
with impunity for ever.

Walkers ascend
faint in austere air;
divers dive
staggering in excess.
They make their choices and pay for them.

But the breathless in hospital beds
have no choices; a graph
charts nightly rides they are called on
to higher and higher terrain
until that Gothic castle by the waterfall
swings down its draw-bridge and the moat is crossed,
and the rest of the story
means turning parchment so tender
a breath would dissolve it.

JOAN FRY

Love's Insight

Take me, accept me, love me as I am;
Love me with my disordered wayward past;
Love me with all the lusts that hold me fast
In bonds of sensuality and shame.
Love me as flesh and blood, not the ideal
Which vainly you imagine me to be;
Love me, the mixed-up creature that you see;
Love not the man you dream of but the real.
And yet they err who say that love is blind.
Beneath my earthy, sordid self your love
Discerns capacities which rise above
The futile passions of my carnal mind.
Love is creative. Your love brings to birth
God's image in the earthiest of earth.

ROBERT WINNETT

A Fragment

Footsteps outside the
window, the tread of
feet on gravel, the
visitors who pause

and go their way,
their unanswered knock
echoing in the empty hall
way of our hearts. Left alone

we measure distance.
Casting the stone
into the heart's well
and counting the moments

until the distant echo tells
how far we are apart.
How lonely passions
separate us. This continuing
drama of our love.

GEOFFREY SMITH
from *Landscapes of the Heart*

Life is for Living

not for chasing the past
or courting the future,
passing, sightless,
through today's avenues,
the landscape of a face,
the season's poetry,

not for braving the world
from a fireside seat,
leaving unchallenged
mountain peaks and rapids,
the fickle mood of oceans,
the desert's mirages,

not for building castles
on technicolour dreams,
confining nightmares to dungeons,
fear to watch-towers,
the sound of chapel-bells
to the last rites.

For living
is feeling life's sweat on your brows
at noon,
its lips on your cheeks at sunset.
It is exploring the unexplorable
and searching for the
Unsearchable.

It is learning how to walk free
in human chains, and how not to drown
in the high seas of suffering.
It is loving and caring and dancing at the fair,
and — in its masterclass — discovering
how to play one's last tune
with a smile.

MARIANNE MACKINNON

Wisdom

On a night like this I could wish for wisdom,
To sit outside my kitchen door
In the long twilight hours, draining my glass
And offering my companions more.
What could be better . . . ?
The breeze in our light summer clothing
And blowing the pages of our open Bibles,
Speaking of this world that came from nothing.

PETER MARSHALL
First published in *Christian*

After Love

'When this is all over . . . ,' we said,
and laughed and made that bed;
made other things seem trivial
and unenduring, lying there joking and seeming equal.

Yet so often now we are like strangers
guilty of acts committed in darkness.
Preferring not to talk we notice
how uneven the body is

in sleep and lie and listen to thoughts
which have no hope of finding voice,
even in these moments
after love, after everything is done, less tense.

Outside the sky is vacant, lost,
at random. As we turn and shift to rest
with slow and separate movements
the wind bleats at our door, and sounds human.

ANTHONY WILSON

Friends and Acquaintances

Whether to the music of guitars,
Daylight clatter or the forest's withering,
The thought that God is here
Sanctifies our moments.
Unwrapping each shining hour
In my heart's attic,
I enfold with the tenderest prayer
All those whose hands I have held,
Lives which with my own have made a garland.

Little Boy Dawdles on the Way to School

Little boy in grey
Groomed for the term's first day
With hateful cap (a little askew)
He wobbles along the wall.
Sun chases rain from pavements
Which played at being windows.
How brightly the flowers sing
As he makes xylophones of railings,
Goes out of his way
To kick a can the length of the street,
Carelessly scuffing immaculate feet,
Frightening a cat from its dustbinned domain.
He reaches the gate, the bell already ringing.
Asked why he is late
Says he stopped to hear the flowers singing.

LYDIA MASKELL

from *Rubella's Child*

I had a child. Too young to flutter, yet
she makes her presence felt in other ways —
a craving for ice-cream. Did that upset
my skin and cause the rash? The sickness phase
subdued, enchanted moments when she first
stretched out a hand and tiny fingers pressed
as soft as damsel wings or bubbles burst
against the pulsing confines of her nest.
My pinioned bird. She's ten years old today,
still seeks the padded limits of her room.
With damaged brain, no hearing, sight, I pray
that love not guilt pervades that sunlit womb?
Rubella's child, I think my heart would break
except I must continue for your sake.

TONI ALLFREY

Young Man of Sorrows

The under-sized young man, with rare
unusual fingers, showing foreshortened
ends and rudimentary nails,
whose eyes were squinting and uneven
under reluctant lids,
with ample, epicanthal folds,
whose brain-power, so they said, was only
seventy per cent of normal,
turned his face from me, as I
questioned him, and wept.
Reports said that he 'needs more practice
in mixing, especially with the
opposite sex', and his angry father,
long ago, had already
forbidden masturbation.
As he cried and searched for a handkerchief,
I thought again that he might have
been me, me him, with those
peculiar fingers, that strange, sad
appearance, making him, with children
or grown-ups, a person to be
bullied, mocked and persecuted.
This crucifixion will last beyond the
ninth hour, and the darkness
when the thunder came, and the tombs opened,
for he is trapped within that shattered
temple of a body, unworshipped and
unworshipping,
until his time is done.

BILL ALLCHIN

Cancer Victim

A cadaver on the pillow smiles in delight.
In self-aware haste I proffer flowers
Messages and love, glad that the fight
is running still. Your warm strong grasp
Belies the faintest beginning rasp of death.
Then words drop defaulting in the air,
From dark-ringed eyes comes a glazing stare,
A harpy's hand picks at your teeth
And twists the last wisps of fading hair.

In desperation I scrabble to control
A boulder crashing through my mind
Uprooting wildly memories of all
Your scholarship and gracious wit.
You flicker back and wilt and then return
Laboriously to ask for friends
Responding with habitual keen concern.
I cherish this gift, deleting the sight
Of your harsh racked face, glad to reaffirm
the hermit-crab existence of your soul.

                                        SUE JAMES

Regards from India

Brown eyes fix
On a distant point
Way above my head:
    You see straight
    Through me, to things
I cannot see —
Thank God!

I would affiliate with you,
But all I have
Is a photograph,
And that is not enough
To make of us
True friends.

Yet in your sea of nakedness
You took time to smile
At a lens,
The camera-extension
Of my affluence.
While my afflatus here
Could not play cool
Upon your cheek,
In the tactile heat
The camera stole a smile.

    Trailing half-lame brothers
    In a convoy of innocence,
    You cannot inculcate
    Beyond your meagre frame.
Space
    Separates us too well:
    How may I not betray you?
And, having said that,
    How in Hell
Will I find you?

MARIO PETRUCCI

Ms Martha Ophelia   (for Delia Smith, an ex-Martha)

'There's rosemary, that's for remembrance.'
Also for roast lamb.

Drowning in sauce,
A kitchen Ophelia
(Housewife to Hamlet),
Not going mad,
Just coping with household
Demands and a job,
Gets exhausted
From gift-wrapping Christmas.

A practising Martha,
Who martyrs herself
To domestic perfection
And personalized notes,
Misses Jesus.

How happy the wife
Whose dedicate life
Is a kitchen utensil.
Each daily routine
Puts a sheen
   and a kiss
On the altar of tidiness.
Bliss is the ending
Of Christmas.

Not next year, not again,
Ms Martha Ophelia,
Jesus has come
To sit next to cleanliness.
Likes to be listened to,
Doesn't mind mess,
Eats Irish stew.

K. LLOYD-THOMPSON

For Edith Stein

(Later Sister Benedicta of the Cross; student of St John of the Cross; died in the gas chambers of Auschwitz.)

Intellectual Jewess in nun's clothing,
Studying her little saint and listening
For the call to come when all her house was hushed
To lead her where no other presence might appear;
In the dark night of her soul she aspired to Being
Oblivious of the Aryan fist upon the door.

Stripped of her Carmelite robes and packed inside
A sweating, fearful wagon-load of death,
She broke bread with her loved and alien kin
And drank with them the wine of suffering.

For forty days this pilgrim Israelite
Trudged praying through the Auschwitz wilderness
While the despairing waters swung to let her pass.

Above, in her dark night, there shone no star
To illuminate a huddled weeping world;
Until one morning in a gas-filled room
She heard the singing of a nightingale
And saw the slopes of Carmel rise to meet
The Golden Sun upon the promised hills.

MICHAEL IVENS
from 'Another Sky'

The Anchoress

She stays a mile from here
The anchoress,
Wrapped in ancient stone:

We leave food by her door
— Lean times a hard
Haul — but we are proud
of our pale one.

All the iron-
Cradling winter out of sight
She prays
For our ills: come the green softs

I see her stride wind-
Quick; the seeking strangers again
Pass by up the hill.

VUYELWA CARLIN

To the nunnery:

*A cerebration on
the Pope's visit to Britain, 1982*

A wing-mirror glance
to the outside lane
for a rampant M4 flash:

3 nuns transfixed
in a white Chevette,

and winking it madly to Heaven.

KEITH PLEASE

For the Bishop of Sokoto

He is an old man; his body stoops,
And his walk is a slow shuffle; his hands
Are too large to manage and hang somewhat
Bewildered at his sides; his face too is large,
Too heavy for the scrawny corded neck, streaked
And pitted by years and hard weather; the eyes
Always fixed on something distant
Unable to focus on anything near, and
The rusty voice not quite talking to you.

His clothes seem haphazard, strange:
Horny feet in purple rubber thongs;
Khaki trousers showing knobby ankles and
Almost skinless shins; a dirty white bouba and
Of course a cross, black wood
With smooth-limbed silver Christ.

How does he manage, this old Bishop
Of Sokoto, for his dim eyes whether
Distant or near see filth and bodies
Fragmented; he must watch wars, police
Torture, find everywhere, lovelessness.

Yet in spite of atoms, cold
Causation, an eroded earth and moon
Desecrated, he clings to a Jewish
Activist as God and knows
That this life leads
               Inevitably to
                          Eternal bliss.

Already, perhaps, he is a boy again,
His horny feet smooth in a whispering stream,
Beech leaves thick about his thoughtless head, sun
Dripping from his nakedness, Africa
And God yet far away.
                       I go into
The road again, pass the shuttered church, turn
From the town onto sun-scorched hill
And pray, in my arrogance, to Something
For the Bishop of Sokoto but halt
Halfway and try to turn my prayer to those of us
Who see the suffering but cannot believe;
Instead words confuse with whitening stone
Scattered as bone from some unknown
Skeleton on this useless hill —
So I return to the mission and drink
Warm beer with Father Peter until
Light is gone.

WILLIAM SANFORD

Caritas

She has lived
you can see it in her face
loving that left her with
marks of a thousand sorrows

She has lived
in ways the world judges
unsuitable
unlovely
unacceptable

She has lived
life to overflowing
in fearful risk-filled
encounters with freedom

She has loved
broken painful caring
for others in that world
Not always worthy
or suitable characters
(people in need are often
unbeautiful, unloved, unclean)

She has lived
you can see it in her eyes
gazing in certainty
of pain and joy and wonder
at the world's being

And the lines of her loving
and the clarity of her vision
and the effort of her living
hurt in her healing heart
She has lived.

JEAN CLARK

The Ascent of Man

I believed in Easter
because my grandma's simnel cake
seemed wonderfully indisputable —
round and solid as a stone.
My grandma's marzipan, glued
with apricot jam,
lay in cross-hatchings over the top
just begging to be peeled away
on the sly.

My grandad ate the cake
but didn't go to church.
Each year the spring pulled his curly kale
up like rabbits out of a hat.
In his garden I found skeleton leaves,
and held their frailty up
for the sun to shine through.

When my grandad died, my dad
planted a canary rose tree,
which flowered yellow
during the days around his death
until the wind bowed
its crown down and broke its trunk.

On the South Downs, that rise up
from the graveyard,
the Long Man can be seen for miles about.
Part of the hillside, he's carved
anonymously into the chalk to show us
a white shape of humanity
through the green turf:
a bold outline, leaning
slightly, on a chalk-drawn stick.

CLARE SNOOK

For M . . .

Since I was fourteen
Christ mattered to me.
I cannot say he intervened
but when the dancing horses of my life
spun out of control
I looked for him
standing by the engine with oily fingers.

Now I am no longer young
— and perhaps a little worn —
he hugs me
and dances
and there is lightness in his arms
and there is lightness in his way.
And when I look for him
(as now I often do)
is it sacrilege to say
Christ has a look of you?

MARGARET COOK

Friend

she still has an apple's good looks
plumping her rosiness
round a wholesome core

blithe since blossom time
she hoarded sunshine in her face
and let the dull days pass

now she'll grace these mellow months
till the trusted hand
cups her from the tree.

A.H. SNOW

Even Rain

Today the lucid mumble and the brave
Send messages to pave their way.
Smiles of the outgoing dangle precariously
Whilst the shy glance up to glance away.
Neighbours stand a foot further from the fence,
But not from reverence,
Faces are replaced by flowers.
Tomorrow, when you are more composed,
They will come in ones and twos.
Even rain, embarrassed from the sky,
Drops soft sporadic showers.

HEATHER MASSIE

Travelling Light

Happily now
I have less use for luggage;
no longer weighted down
am free to travel lightly,
to fill my eyes,
and empty out my pockets.

Happily now
I have no need to bother
my foolish head with questions;
can safely substitute
the trodden earth
for fruitless speculation.

Happily now
I know that I know nothing.
My eventual learning
will be as new,
breathtaking,
as the first steps of children.

KATHLEEN HERBERT
from *Travelling Light*

The Visitation

I have been for too long a frequenter
of quayside and harbour,
                a keel-hauler of men's souls;
                a seeker-out of stagnant pools
and the sacred groves of mistletoe;
of the god that causes moss to grow
                on the underside of felled trees —
                an interpreter of others' melodies.
But since that visitation, when the angel spoke
out of the darkness in which we all partake,
                I have become, as it were, a tremulous reed
                blown through by the word of God.

IAN PARKS
from *Three Songs of Caedmon*

Pastoral Encounter

Once
I   saw
An old man
Gently crying
For no clear reason.
I was touched by his grief,
And asked him to share with me
The   source   of   his   tribulation.
He told me I lacked tact and manners
For stamping on his chance to mourn alone,
The final right left in an Old Folks' Home,
Where   all   emotions   are   untidy
And must be cleared away — or else
Matron would be most upset
And prone to take action
Of unpleasant sort.
All this he said
Without sound,
His eyes
Dead.

B.R. STEVENS

A Casting-Off

She sits and briskly knits, her needles clack
And grimly add the seconds of her life.
Her head is bent so she won't see his chair
Whose vacancy insists 'no longer wife'.

She chooses factory-wound wool, as skeins
Would underline his absence, sharpen need
For deft controlling thumbs to gather threads,
His held-out arms that always took the lead.

And at her knee she taught me purl and plain;
She'd pick up stitches, undo and put right
My every tangle; tackle garter, rib ·
Till lymph and blood and bile snapped off her light.

Her knitting-bag was needle-sharp, and full —
Unfinished work, and ball on ball of wool.

ANGELA TOPPING
from *Dandelions for Mothers' Day*

Requiem for David Lewis: A man of faith

Early autumn you chose for dying,
days when the sun burst through hilariously
after a short-lived, indecisive haze,
just like your moodiness melting to merriment
through repartee to mimicry or anecdotal fling.
Often you'd set yourself to harvesting ideas,
then rake and stack them deftly for your store
— tossing the gleanings of your wit to captivated friends —
sometimes you'd root out tares among the crop
— patches of joylessness or fuss or bigotry —
working the ground till it returned your smile.
Continuing colour filled your autumn fields:
you had the enchanter's gift of making others grow
until they flowered in the climate of your cheer.

History will never see you as a sculptured saint;
you missed perfection with the rest of men,
hastening to battle in the brushwood of debate,
pitchforking praise or blame or thwacking through dissent,
yet always mindful of the rising grain,
assessing it for fitness on the threshing floor,
while you consistently proclaimed eventual weal
beyond all hazards of the toil-worn years.
It seemed appropriate that death stooped tenderly
— not rousing you from sleep —
and with compassionate grasp carried the harvest home.

ELIZABETH HAMILTON - JONES

Remembrance Sunday Find

A Second World War heroine:
tortured by the Gestapo
her toe-nails removed —
>   I could not read all —
>   but still refusing to give
>   the desired information.
How few such women must remain?
How few such men and women
can there ever have been?
>   When asked, thirty years on
>   how she did it, how she conquered the pain,
>   replied simply.

'There were trees
outside the prison.
I concentrated on these.
>   And the knowledge
>   it was early summer . . .
>   death, when it comes, will be like home.'

JULIE WHITBY

For Benjamin Moloise:
hanged in Pretoria, Friday, 18 October 1985

Life springs from death; and from the graves of patriot men and women spring living nations (Padraic Pearse)

Moloise the world stands
to observe a silence for you
for your people
        together we bow our head
        around that stadium of suffering
        your death now our bereavement your courage
        our abhorrence of every repressor
of those who would attempt
to hide freedom in a cloud of tear-gas
to beat justice to its knees with the *sjambok*
to dangle Africa from a white noose
to bury in quicklime the poetry of youth
        and the world's silence runs like blood
        it fills their sad swimming pools
        seeps into verandahs and through bricks
        it hangs on their bullwire it
        creeps across the gold vaults
and deepens
it becomes a scream
it enters our conscience too
with the wood of your coffin the
soft weight Benjamin of your life
as we take turns shouldering your remains
mourning yes but inspired as well at seeing
the spirit being true to itself and ideal
brandished like a burning spear
        so that when they hanged you we all became black
        the hangman peers and hides and looks at his list
        we Irish could have warned him no grave
        would go deep enough to hold you
        no more than it held Pearse
        no more than it can hold any patriot
and though they tried to get rid of you
in the early hours when the world was asleep
the fools
they did not see your soul breaking over Africa
over the whole earth dawning behind their digging
        Benjamin son of days.

Mrs Ned

she would waddle out from their stone kitchen
gently on slippers her bandaged leg
giving inwards as if under the soft
bulk in the navy shopcoat
usually calling back at some of the *childer*
poor Marion never too far away
or Barney Thomas our pal

every year she'd have their shop window in flowers
with candles and a Sacred Heart for the procession
and my mother cried a long time
the evening Mrs Ned died.

DESMOND EGAN
from *Collected Poems*

World Issues

Lent '88

The film primes opinions. Freedom
Is our cry. The long body, prone, brown,
Is Biko. The policemen are evil.
There is a plea in our hearts for pardon
For the complicitous six of Sharpeville.
We want the Afrikaaners to lose at power-tennis —
Their guns and riot-shields will not protect
For ever. In time they will go under.

The photograph, next morning, is of Ulster.
The body, no actor's, supine, bloody,
Is a British soldier's, torn
At a political funeral, like Biko's.
There is revenge in our hearts, against
Any who were in that riot. We want
Better shields, effective police. The SAS.

There is too much leisure for opinion
In our English flower-gardens.
Our hearts riot; the words in them
Tangle, like ornamental ivy —
Justice, lust, compassion, Barabbas.
We are at the worst station of the Cross —
The one at which we feel our reflexes fail.

CHRISTOPHER SOUTHGATE

Cristo Guerillero

'God who sweats in the street,
God with a sunburnt face.'
— Nicaraguan Mass, Carlos Mejia Godoy

'It was the gospel of Jesus Christ
That made a Marxist out of me.'
— Father Ernesto Cardenal

The guerillero came down from the mountain
His tongue was the book of exodus
eyes open wide as gospels
He was in need of a shave

Clothed in a red T-shirt and blue denim jeans
baseball cap, and bearing the stigmata on
his feet, hands and side

Needing help as only a saviour can,
he placed concepts that were like
plastic explosives against the military
installations
that we had set up around our hearts.

Fears fled before him like vanquished
Guardia Nacional.

One Campensino, a man called Tomas
didn't . . . couldn't believe at first
but once he had touched
the beautiful wounds
he knew, and was
Radicalised by Love.

BILL LEWIS
First published in *Rage Without Anger*

Woman in a Tableau
(after an incident in the Sahel region reported by a UNICEF official)

dust colours her face
                        nightmare
drought
                        water polluted
the choice between
                        giving her child watery mud
and letting him die
                        seeing the choice
over and over
                        telling her hands
becoming the choice
                        giving the baby poisoned water
his tongue burning now
                        forever against hers.

KATHERINE GALLAGHER
from *Passengers to the City*

The Unemployed

the cormorants
                a black dole queue
stand on Marsden Rock
                totally unemployed

there are still the working ones
the kittiwakes mewing busily
around the rocks in the sea

but for the cormorants there is
nothing to do
                one flaps off slowly
and another returns
                with no news of work
the rest just stand around.

RODNEY WARD
First published in *Christian*

Vigil for Peace: Brixton 1981

Only the usual handful of embarrassed Christians
standing around, not sure how obviously
they should appear to pray —
eyes up, eyes down — whether to grin at friends
who nudged late into the circle,
wondering how to rise above
the roar of evening traffic round the island.

Somehow the policemen made it seem worthwhile —
a large green busload, brought in from the suburbs,
just in case the sisterhood had hidden half-bricks
in their handbags, or the charismatic clergy
turn from tongues of fire to petrol bombs.
But while, across the road, they played
at cards, or dozed, a silence deepened.

Candles were lighted all around the rosebed.
Passing children who stopped by to stare
were caught up, sharing a curious quiet.
So, the evening darkened; street lamps
turned the trees to yellow, candles brightened,
and the silence grew; until the chiming
of the Town Hall clock plumbed through,

and people turned to shake hands,
talk a little, then walk quietly away,
— not wanting to claim anything,
but just returning through scarred streets,
past shops sold up and gone, leaving the idle bus
to drive its bored young men back home.

TONY LUCAS
First published in *Brixton Mortar*

Red Nose Day

mode I: Ode to a red nose
        To what shall I compare thee
        Red nose?
        I dare not wear thee
        on the Piccadilly Line

        Red nose
        What a powerful *agent provocateur* you are!
        Red nose
        blow the comparisons
        I salute you.

mode II: Comic relief in heaven — or is it laughter?
        Clutching my red nose in my pocket,
        Questions I can ask:
        Would God wear a nose for such a cause?
        Christ the Clown
        our fool for God's sake
        the only one
        to wear a nose on red nose day
                Good Friday
        for the sake of Ethiopia
        Yes — and much more.

ROSIE WATSON

AIDS Victim

Positive, there's no doubt.
The confirmation set him back ten years or more
To rendezvous in pubs, dark mats and soft lights
hung above the fruit machine,
where whisperings and beer frothed his downfall.

Trips to see the sea on Sunday
Waffles and saunterings down the cobbled street
back to his place.
Touchings, gestures befitting women —
strutting peacocks around the television
until their love collapsed on the carpet.

The agony came later,
the agony of guilt locked in an earring,
festooned upon his face the unsaid sins,
the signs of other love pinned on the nurse's breast.
She gave him water when he called
and in the night she listened.
Like Mary, she had the better part.

MARTIN EGGLETON

Half Voice

It is the beginning
And orchestral suite
Following shapes created
By celestial breeze
Shakes harmony from the wheat
And all humankind are free
To eat.
It is the day after
and we find
Edge of time brushed
With corruption
And men — faces flushed
With greed —
Begin to covet the seed.

It is today
And Christian thought Dutch-barned
In its comfort
Moves not beyond
Personal experience
Incapable of passing through fence
Of undressed fears
Dividing field from field
And half-raised voices
Are pressed into silence of the years
Gathering increased yield
Where we harvest
But shadows of the corn
And hear but echo of the song
Caught upon thorn of circumstance
And as we break the bread
Of conscience
And dance the dance
Of wine-cupped responsibility
We feel hunger of the unfed
And before our eyes appears
Hidden pain of the man
From Galilee
And pilgrims of Amritsar
Mecca and beyond
Watch in silence
As shears of truth
Scythe through our sleep
And awakening we weep
Our Jerusalem tears.

PAT ISIORHO

The Holy Innocents

O World, wide world, grown up,
Grown up and weary of the day,
Let not this moment
Nor the cry depart —
Till all the broken buds,
The tender and the helpless ones,
The Innocents in all our guilty places,
Are loved and mourned
As they are loved and mourned
In the open arms
Of Christ.

A.J. LEWIS
from *Whitsunday Rain*

Poppies

On Sunday, 8 November an IRA bomb exploded at the Remembrance Day
parade at Enniskillen, Northern Ireland. Eleven civilians were killed and many
more injured.

SUNDAY.   A black umbrella protrudes from rubble,
a dilapidated poppy wreath among the
brick barrage and blood.
The shape of bodies bagged in death's finality.
Ambulance, police, fire-engine, army;
sirens pronouncing tragedy.

TUESDAY.   In the black drear of November, exposed tree
structures knit branches to hold bright air.
Memory sprinkled from a dried poppy casket
scatters grains of unfulfilment.
Empty bodies encased in wood are lowered into earth
whose map reference is Northern Ireland
where remembering is as normal as rain.

SUE MOULES
First published in *Poetry Wales* 1989

Non-believing Cybernetics

A million prayers,
stored within the hardware
of his head,
provide instant intercession
on seeing
ribcage child,
rickety cleaner,
roadside crash.

Such throughput
cuts against the grain
of his disbelief,
upholds the Creator
as programmer
of his data base.

ERNEST DEWHURST

Prisoners of Conscience

Remember them, under our feet
Their clenched and unremitting nightmare
Sunken wells of eyes, frayed ropes of spirit
A child's handful of stars in their square of sky
But their cries, clotted with bloodshot tears
Are splinters of the great Tree, the first Thorn.

KENNETH C. STEVEN

Two Birthdays

The door swung shut behind me
To leave me in the street.
The shoppers, rolling cars and gliding bikes
A silent film
Before those pounding words.

Those careful, measured phrases
Which measured off my life —
Professionally final sentences
Which sentenced hope
To send it to its cell.

Two years is all — two birthdays —
I know the secret thing
That man is not supposed to know at all —
The time at which
The limousine will call.

But as the silent driver,
Unhearing, does his job,
I'll strain to hear an old familiar voice
So full of life,
The voice of tombless Christ.

And when the job is over,
I'll find myself at home,
The fearsome words, the street, will then become
The dream that fades
As sunlight floods the room.

PETER F. JONES
First published in *Christian*

Le Dormeur du Val: Antrim

(after Rimbaud)

Sunrise; a stream from some distant spring
stirs in undergrowth like a waking child; brown
bubbles with silver bubbles on their back bring
life to primroses, narcissi, vetch; a man
lies in a froth of sunshine, his face down
in the water, drinking; dew is a dust
of night light on his back and last year's dun
leaves are nestling him; he is still, as if he had just
slaked a long thirst. Nearby a wren
makes morning music; through a banquet hall
of sunshafts, reeds, the boles of trees, tense
urgency of traffic on a road. It is cold
in the wood but he is not shivering, his head
in the water and the mosses stained bright red.

JOHN F. DEANE
from 'Road, with Cypress and Star'

Art

Venice Triptych

I.   Before going into St Mark's out of the rain

    I took Sylvia to see the Doge, first
    In the Ducal Palace: he wasn't there.
    Rain spouted from the roof and slapped the bare
    Buttocks of the courtyard. With our eyes pursed,
    We tried, in his absence, to pierce the gloom. Thirst
    For one painter's vision lured us to stare
    Beyond the visual at Europa's share
    Of the bull's affection. Veronese burst
    Out in breast flesh and a cow looking on
    Lowed in complicity. 'He's in the square,'
    She called from a bull's-eye. 'There's a pigeon
    On his wrist pecking crumbs.' But he was gone
    When we got down. 'You're seeing things! Swear
    You won't be raped by that bull, religion!'

II.   Bellini's Virgin, Santa Maria dei Frari

    It's the angels that worry me, playing
    Their instruments inaudibly until
    The concierge closes the church. 'You will
    Have to come back after lunch.' So saying,
    He locks and shuffles off. 'Leave them praying,
    All the saints.' All concierges shuffle
    And all saints pray. We do up our duffel
    Coats against the October wind. Weighing
    The pros and cons of trattoria fare
    We temporize, buy stuffed olives, fresh rare
    Thin slices of meat and a length of bread. Soon
    We're eating and downing wine in honour
    Of one who's waiting for us, Madonna
    Of the sacristy, keeping the angels in tune.

III.   Out in the Lagoon

    There are five of us, leaning together
    And held round the nape — also the torso —
    By metal stays. Backs braced to the weather
    We stand, our knees wet and our feet more so!

Now if one of us loses his footing
We take the strain. If your falling brother
Leans on you bodily, you're off putting
The world to rights. We're helping each other
And the world passes us by in its boats:
Steamers, gondolas with outboard motors,
Noah's ark — in fact, anything that floats.
We are not five of your floating voters!
Persuasive waves browbeat our reflections.
We're gathering moss, and there's no defections.

CHRISTOPHER PILLING

Pietà (On seeing Michelangelo's sculpture)

They let me
            hold Him
                        in my arms,
Across my legs
            I felt
                        the weight
Of my son's
            bruised and
                        bleeding form.
His pierced head
                with its matted
                                    hair
I held close
        against
                my breast
Cradling it there.
                    Hungrily I held Him
                                    to myself,
And down
        within
                my soul
Deep groaning grew —
As once again
                my body knew
The pain
        and wrench
                of labour.

But now
        it was not
                Joy
That came
        to birth
But Sorrow
        wailing
                in the light,
Torn from
        my leaden
                body —
Offspring
        of grief
                and fear,
'Eloi, Eloi, lama sabachthani' —
Like Him,
        I cried out
                in my pain.
Then I looked down
And saw
        that God
                was here —
Here,
    in all the blood
                and sweat,
Here,
    in the midst
                of blasphemy
    and sin —
        God was —
And I could weep
And I shall sing!

LYN JENNINGS

Gloria

(Fourteenth-century Service Book, Yorkshire Museum)

Staves are flecked with curving lines
As he leans and bends to place the pen
Obedient to the angle of each note,
Hearing them rise
To the ears of Mary
Who kneels where the two vaults intersect
And smiles.

LYDIA HARRIS

Icon

Not that beauty is absent,
Though the face fastidious,
The nose too aquiline,
Flaked and peeled to disenchant,
While raised eyes set in suffering
Add no further adornation;

Yet, seen in the reflected light
Of offering and ornament,
The pigments live; as we shall
Who believe in the resurrection,
In an instant resplendent,
Like stained-glass quickened by sunlight.

TOM McGONIGLE

Pietà

It is not was not can not be
   of flesh
      it is was will be
stone:
the cold still rock, greyed marble wrenched
from mountainside, hauled through
the ravaged forests to a city room, there
hammered, chiselled, chipped
by vicious lust-stained muscles to
that sharp and angled thing she holds —
she — another piece of rock, hammered down
to folds of question mark
forced to position of lament before
the naked wounded one.

WILLIAM SANFORD

The Icon of Our Lady

Preoccupied, she
Has no eyes for the child,
But looks deep within
Herself, wondering:
Is this all I get
For giving myself to God?
Doubts, fears, strange promises;
An aging husband;
This clamorous child
Perched precariously
On my breast, with the face
Of an old priest, handing
Me a divisive gospel
Which will break my heart.

What can I do but
Mother him, feed him,
Wash him, teach him to pray,
Love him, and let him go
His own way to his Father?

Perhaps for servants,
For the poor in spirit,
God's way is just this:
Nothing more;
But no less.

DOUGLAS COWLING

Cimabue Crucifix on Tour

We are astonished, seeing the face so marred,
the body blistered, paint all flaked away.
The sponsors seek to lessen our dismay
with detailed facts on laminated card.

It has become an object to discuss —
express our horror at such devastation,
debate the merits of the restoration,
admire the form, and how a sinuous

body cuts the rigid frame, first flower
of a humanistic spring. Thus, blunted
of its splendour, we are not confronted
by a force of spiritual power.

And while we analyse, why not enquire
how our theologies have multiplied,
creed, canon, doctrine, all have ramified,
where once was just the Word that burnt like fire?

Is this what we must do to God — abuse,
consume the flesh, despoil the radiant face,
and let a broken form deflect the grace,
dissect his glory for the fragments we can use?

TONY LUCAS

Petrus

Sculptor sees striving Seraph with stretched wings
Struggle: strict the straitness of his prison.
By canny craft he frees him.
How is it that he sees him?
How beckon into being but by Risen
Life, indwelling insight, God who springs
Singing when he sees us,
— And seeing, loves and frees us —

As once within unyielding block a Rock
Surly stubborn Simon he discerned:
Marbled in the Law
Christ cruxed Cephas saw —
Knew he, many bitter lessons learned
Would stand tooled forth first Shepherd of the flock —
So struck the chisel-blow
Which freed his friend to grow.

JULIE SINCLAIR

Crucifixion — a Triptych by Francis Bacon 1965

Deaf-mute walls without windows
menacing the eye,
wall-to-wall fitting office-grey
binding the unbindable;
the bare bones of efficiency
uphold the unspeakable.

Bound by the name of crucifixion,
paint smears mutate,
from blood to paint
from paint to blood.
From shrieks of pain and broken bone,
tormented flesh daubs paint.

   No sign's didactic, the artist said,
   uplift dries out like unwrapped bread.

The central figure hangs —
a trophy on a wall;
arms bound in splints and bandaged head
upturned, converted, with Saint Paul.

From where the legs and the belly would be
guts and offal spread.
On one side of the crucified —
the crucified in bed.
On the other side of the crucified —
the crucified on a chair.

    Our fear of prophesy no longer fed —
    three people torn as one to carrion.
        For God's sake no sermon, the artist said.

And a bruised naked woman waddles away
like a plucked and gutted bird of prey
towards the oven.
Watched by two men.
Respectful panamas help shade their eyes
from decency. They shield their skin-full
in suburban suits, black knotted ties.

Few human signs this far survive
the party arm-band, the partisan rosette.
The bogus human rots while still alive.

    Our daily bread as voyeurs stinks in our head.
        Please, no parallel, no parable, the artist said.

DENNIS HAWKINS

Cabbages

(after a painting by Paul Waplington)

I saw a picture once —
I remember it well.
There was a bereaved old man,
faceless and grey,
sitting,
or rather, slumped,
by the side of his allotment.

There were sheds, or something,
in the background,
and the rest was just
cabbages,
only larger than life.
And the soil looked
purple
with his grief.

I could have cried.
I suppose the cabbages
were important.
They'd be all he'd got
left.

Of course,
you couldn't have hung it
on your dining-room wall,
or else
you'd never have eaten
your dinner.

I can't seem to forget
that picture.
It was kind of beautiful.

But sad.

JOAN ROWBOTTOM

Sunflowers

Earth-coloured people, potato
eaters, we too look up, expecting
new colours in the sky;

gravestones in the churchyard already
taunt us, flaunting our names
where dandelion tubers grow
big as fists. The man

who gave his canvasses as clothing
for the poor, had hoped, like us,
for brighter colours, and had filled the world
with sunflowers, gifts of yellow light,
simplicities, like Japanese prints, deft
individual strokes of paint for bridge
or tree or man. But night

threatened; his hatband was a bush
of lighting candles; he tried to cry
but no tears came; he painted a field
coloured like angry sunflowers where crows
were gathering, where earth-coloured paths
led suddenly off the canvas; his yellows

grew too hot, and the sky filled
with a black rain (though otherwise
the day was fair); if you were to take a gun now
against those crows before the violent
mistral dries your brain
to ice, ending the Japanese
dream, Hiroshima, Nagasake,
earth-coloured people, who tried to cry . . .

JOHN F. DEANE
First published in *Road, with Cypress and Star*

Leonardo's Last Supper

Voluble Milanese crammed in a tin-can tram
Clutching shopping and children
Converse in shouts.
It seems very jolly,
If noisy,
To live in Milan.

Pushing desperately towards the exit
(*Inglese? Inglese?*)
I squeeze out into a dusty square
Where, in a plain stone building
Is a large bare room
Like an empty barn,
On one wall a pale flaking mural.

A long table is painted across this wall.
Twelve restless men are having a meal
Behaving in a noisy Milanese manner.
In the centre,
A thirteenth man.
Still.
Already in another world.

BRIGID SOMERSET

Chartres Cathedral

The spires lean
into the air
touch the blue inside
of the sky

lightly
a philosophy

a cathedral
about to lift the world
off its knees.

KATHERINE GALLAGHER
from *Passengers to the City*

Apostle Windows

JOHN

In winter he runs on stars and a road of moonlight
That frosts the window underneath his feet;
Makes his young face haggard, his robe white.

And sometimes in the lamplight from the street
He races down the long dim afternoons
Through rain that soaks and darkens like a threat.

It is a long way to the tomb.
Too far for a man to run in isolation.
Hoping, not knowing, agitated by rumour and some

Desperate, quivering elation.
Through history he has run towards the dawn,
the grave-cloths cast aside, the implication.

JUDAS

Never in any church have I seen you;
never on windows or on squat misericords or carved
even in the dimmest cobwebbed corner of a crypt;
and if I did, you would only be hanging;
or clutching your silver ransom, or offering
that treacherous kiss. They never have anything good
to say of you, and who can blame them?
Heretics are worse than unbelievers
in the eyes of the betrayed.
Still, I wonder how you would look, how they might
portray you — whether the beard would be swarthy,
the eyes shifty, aslant —
because there is a roundel here of Christ in Hell,
embracing a man waist-deep in fiery glass
whose medieval face turns up as if in shock.
The features of both are gone; scrubbed by history
to a blaze of sunlight, as if that moment
transcended all colour, all the
glazier's power to create.
Perhaps it is something in the kiss that makes me
wonder if they meant it to be you.

CATHERINE FISHER

The Bible

In the Beginning

God laughed,
And the firmament fumed and spluttered with pleasure;
And the sea shook the foam of his hair from his eyes;
And earth was glad.

The sound of the laughter
Was like the swaying and swinging of thunder in mirth;
Like the rush of the north on a drowsy and dozing land;
It was cool. It was clear.

The lion leapt down
At the bleating feet of the frightened lamb and smiled;
And the viper was tamed by the thrill of the earth,
At the holy laughter.

We laughed,
For the Lord was laughing with us in the evening;
The laughter of love went pealing deep into the night:
And it was good.

PAUL BUNDAY
First published in *Christian*

after the flood
Noah lived always in the tension
between the promise of the rainbow
and the memory of choking screams
in the water, the scratching and sliding
of fingernails on the lurching sides
of his Ark.

in the bottle he found some resolution
he drowned the screams again
in an hour or two of forgetfulness, his eyes turned to the earth.

they found him naked and oblivious.
some things within him had not survived
the flood. Some things that did survive
already undermined his pretensions
to a brave new world.

We, his grandchildren, continue his work,
building ever more sumptuous illusions
to drown our struggling awareness

year by year
we are found ever more
naked.

ANDREW M. RUDD

The Conversion of Moses

'Jahweh Sabaoth,
Adonai, Elohim —
what shall I call you,
god, O God?'
said Moses in agony,
Moses trembling,
Moses under the judgement rod.

But the Lord exploded
in glorious laughter.
'I am who I am —
have you got it? Good.
Ask a silly question
and you get a silly answer!'
And Moses smiled
and understood.

SIMON BAYNES
First published in New Fire

Immanuel

Did Adam realise,
Lurking in the bushes full of shame,
What he had lost?
Did Eve remember,
Lying in the sweat of first-birth pain,
The seed of promise almost
Hidden by the sentence?
Maybe not.

Later, others who'd known nothing else,
Not heard him in the garden —
The cracking of small twigs underfoot,
The rustle of grass —
Others met him.
Unexpectedly he came
To Hagar in the desert
And Abraham under the huge trees.
All night Jacob struggled with the glorious stranger.
Moses was afraid at first;
Too bright a burning, too fierce
The heat of holiness.
Yet he became a friend,
Spoke face to face, began
To know as he was known.
Joshua the soldier met his captain;
Even Gideon was commissioned
And one day Manoah's wife
Surprised her husband.
Samuel listened; Daniel saw
At dead of night,
In the stillness,
Such a sight of future days
As threatened sanity.

Meanwhile
In the womb of time
The promise grew. The seed
Took root in humble lime,
Davidic clay;
Began to sprout and bud
In men's minds, almost understood
By some to whom the word came.

They saw it
Growing as a righteous branch;
Unfurled before the nations
Like a banner, bringing distant islands
And scattered peoples
Home.

But they could not see
What lay between.
What lay in straw
And slept
Or cried with hunger.
Could not have foreseen
The unexpectedness of this.

Did Adam watch? And Eve?
And did they weep again,
This time with joy at such
Deliverance?
They had not thought
That he would live with them like this,
Inhabiting the world he made
So finally. Restoring all
Lost hope so permanently.
Coming, as always,
So unexpectedly.
Immanuel.

JUDITH LYONS

Little Prayer for Samson and Delilah

When all virtue
like Samson's Rastafarian locks
lies strewn in pieces about us,
have mercy, Lord,
on those who sleep in weakness
and those who have shorn us of strength.

Like the growing stubble on Samson's head,
let us be renewed to undertake
the phenomenal as matter of course
when we awaken
from the lap of philistine ease.

DIANE KARAY TRIPP

Nativity

They saw my heaving
belly and the doors
slammed, so he dropped
into straw and mud.
It was my own hand
that wiped the blood
from his waxy head.

An old man said I
had given birth to
a sword, but I knew
he had already cut
his way out of me.
Afterwards he healed
me with his warm moist
mouth on my nipple,
I loved him stirring
with his first satisfaction.

He carried the edge through
long years and at last
the sharp blade drove straight
into him. At his death
I wiped blood from his
waxen head, held him
against my breast.

LIZ KIRBY

At Nazareth

A stroke of light. The girl's hand
fending brilliance from her mind.
And afterwards, a slow, decisive
quickening of the wells within her,
palpitations in the universe
of water where the child's form

half understood, half human,
moved and grew. By day
the women gossiped, nodding
at the months inside her belly,
sifting, calculating, crooked
in their grins; at night

the man would throw himself
beside her, scented with the piquant
resins of his trade. Inside their room,
swollen on the bed's hard form,
she'd lie, the child between her palms,
at rest, laid sideways, half asleep

and feel him thrust and prod
against her inner self. He trod
her body's currents, drifting out
towards himself, an image
brilliant on the dark horizons
topped by one dark hill, still far away.

ROGER IREDALE

Between Annunciation and Answer

We do not see anguish on her face
nor feel her involuntary shudder.
But the seconds
between annunciation and answer,
vast, jagged, an insomniac's night,
are time enough to ponder
whether the words riddling her ear
are demonic murmur
or grandiose hallucination.

All we see are momentary puzzlement
laced with a wingbeat of fear
before her hands unclench
and lips part to frame the words,
'Let it be to me . . .'

Does guidance ever come otherwise?
A shudder of disbelief,
then hands outstretched
beneath the spill
of mystery.

DIANE KARAY TRIPP

Nativity

The town was dark and shuttered.
No child cried, nor ox lowed.
From far off, like a whisper of eternity
the ass came, the sharp hooves
parting and spurning the dust,
breaking sleep abruptly as stones on a window.

Who knows how many woke
to the knocking of the man?
Who knows how many staggered, like the innkeeper,
from their hot beds, cursing down the stairs?
Who knows how many sneaked a glimpse
of the commotion and slammed the heart's door?

Maybe the woman, God in her belly,
saw the guilty movements around her,
and, accepting the stable meekly as a slap in the face,
knew in her labour that for all those
there would be room on the green hill,
and room, too, at the white table of the spilled blood.

J. D. GILPIN

The Woman Who Touched
(Matthew 9, Mark 5, Luke 8)

The blood and the bleeding
The pressure and the pain:
Twelve long, long years of burning
And unclean, unclean remain the scars
Of indecent haemorrhage.
Scars that poison body, poison mind
And drain, deplete resources
Money, love
And trust of human kind.
Cheating quacks and useless doctors
Unable to enable
Without skill to still the bleeding
Without love to quench the pain.

Ah, the hem, the hem and
Crack!
The rim of the ring is ripped:
Faith has broken in
Where pressure could not pierce.
And from the transfixed circle flows
The blood and water of Christ's love
And that
Straight replenished from above.

Now Christ, the Master
All perceiving
Sees or feels the gradual diminishing
Of undiminished power.

Power gone.

Though many press on
Their pressure is not noticed
As devoid of single strength.
But one, at length
One pressure came, her hand of faith
And perspicacious Saviour saw it such
And much, much love was in his heart
When turned he round
And bade the woman go
Forever free.

By faith forever cured out in the world
But ever in the circle
Of his love.

MARTIN CRAPPER

The Women

Powerless to effect a rescue,
Not for us
The melodramatic gestures of the men.
If we had swords, would we have acted thus?
No: mutilation's not our kind of game.
But, unlike men, we didn't turn and flee;
We followed at a distance, doggedly,
Mocked by the soldiers, jostled by the crowd . . .
And we were there
To hear that cry that sounded like despair,
We shared her pain
When she held his body in her arms again,
And took her home, and kissed her poor wan face,
Rocked her to sleep at last in our embrace
And waited all the night
And all the Sabbath for the first sad light
Of the ensuing day,
And then, with spices, we were on our way:
Burial and birth we know.
But, as we neared
The place, mist cleared:
We saw the stone rolled back
And hesitated by the yawning black
Mouth, then we went in,
Groping to find only an empty shroud.
Suddenly, there was light: warmth glowed.
We left the cave reborn
And ran home, laughing aloud.

But one stayed behind,
Magdalene. Was it tears that made her blind?
She told us later that she had to stay
Close to the place where her beloved lay.
So she was first to meet him,
To undo the traitor's kiss and greet him.
We thought it right
She should be chosen for delight.
But, when she told the men,
Incredulous, as of us, they jeered and then
Ran off to see for themselves. The rest is told.
But just remember: men recount the story,
We women were the first to see the glory.   JOAN SMITH

The Fifth Rider of the Apocalypse

The meadow will be green and
The horse
Will be white,
Its muzzle thick with pollen
From pods, and pips of light.
The meadow will be green and
The eyes
Cowled in silk,
The wings poised for flight
Of the horse white as milk.
The meadow will be green and
The horse
Unafraid,
The wings extra bright
But the eyes gentian shades.
The meadow will be green and
The winds
Will be right,
The path pale as honey
But the horse will be white.
   Like travellers to Paradise
   with longings overlaid,
The eyes will be steadfast.
The Rider
Unafraid.

GINA RILEY

Christian Images

The spirit of God,
Like an all-consuming flame,
Burns us, heart and soul.

The Dove reminds us
That the Spirit of the Lord
Sets us truly free.

The Gospel of John
Is soaring like an eagle
To the throne of grace.

The Lord, my Shepherd,
Leads me to the green pastures
Beside still waters.

Light in perfect form,
Brilliant blue rose window,
Flame of the Divine.

B. HILDEBRANDT

Times and Festivals

The Indoor Jesus

Jesus is born at the hinge of the year round which
pivot the open season and the shut,
born at the ebb, the inverse climacteric;
for what lives now, survives against the odds,
hibernates, wraps itself in coats and scarves
or rooms with fires. Yet shortly the aconite
will shove its tiny, incredible yellow head
up through a floor, mottled, tiled with frost.

Windows look inward, nuclear families
watch TV, love or quarrel or play together
at Christmas games, until eventually
they draw thick curtains firmly across the night.
Out here among the trees nothing much moves.
The bark of a fox grown bold with hunger echoes
like a mouse gnawing behind the wainscot in
an empty room. In the year's empty quarter
Jesus comes to a cold birth and lifts
like the fragile courageous flower, a head to face
the north face of the hills, uttering
just audibly a promise that the improbable
trick of springtime will be brought off again.

The manger is open to the wind; wolves
howl in the mountains. Soon perhaps
men with foreign swords will come to check
the passports of the immigrants, or maybe
someone will plant a bomb at the cave's mouth
in a carrier-bag, to enforce with TNT
some ideology or other, or they might
snatch the baby for a hostage till
God pays the ransom, dispensing profligate
vanloads of cheap grace so we don't have to pay
the price of our redemption's happy dawn.

The tinsel angel on the Christmas tree
smiles down at our smiling faces, almost we
can fool ourselves that the antique fantasy
of coming home from school to welcoming
arms and supper in the firelight is permanently
the human condition; that warm and secure
life is a succession of lighted rooms

through which we walk to a succession of welcomes till
the last one wraps it up. This angel makes
no mention of the bird, linnet or sparrow
fluttering through the king's banqueting hall
between the dark and the dark, and yet out there
loom the realities that lend our seemings
their vestiges of truth. The path of the bird,
dazzled and faltering, is a kind of limping
protest-march unsponsored on behalf of
the left and the bereft, the hungry and cold;
of those whose voyage on the turbulent
lake among squalls prompts an occasional
a desperate 'Save us we're sinking'. Yes
I know that my redeemer liveth but
through ill-fitting windows the draughts persist.
Pivot the door on its hinge, outwards towards
the world of the aconite and the apple-tree.
Not yule-log, not boar's head, not all our carols
can keep our cosy indoor Jesus warm.

KEVIN NICHOLS
from *Begotten in Silence*

Spring Trees at Pleshey

And can these dry bones live?
these bare boughs sprout green?
In my hand the twigs snap —
no sign of living sap —
and each stalk
is sharp, dry as chalk,
scratches blood
with the hard knot of wood.

And can these dry boughs live?
Yes, since one tree of death
bore love's last breath
   (no harder wood
   no bleaker bough
   no sharper thorn
   we'll ever know)

and flamed with the fruit of Christ's risen body
on the first Good Sunday,
all trees on earth partake this miracle,
proclaim this glory.

Look long, then, here, at this
budding of dead wood:

and in our lives,
however dry or gnarled the grain,
He'll cause the flower of love
to sprout again.

NICOLA SLEE

Lent

And He was led
Out
Into a desert place,
Where there was neither
Right nor left
To go,
And no man else
But He Himself
To know.

Hunger hammered, haunted,
Held
The very stones
His feet did cry
Upon;
Circled searching
Hand and eye,
The tender tongue —
And no bird sang
But lay in shade
Afraid.

He prayed.

Stones were not to be
Bread for company
But word of God He chose;
And hunger wept to know
Such strange repose.

A temple bore He
And a house of high intent
Was His,
The sum of all whose parts
Was praise;
He would not turn
To wanton sorcery
The house of God.

He in stillness knelt
To offer praise —
And each bird stood
Remembering
The apple's wood.

From the high place He looked
Upon the glory of the worlds
That lay about His feet;
The sight was sweet —
He turned upon the tempter:
'Ah, No!
These are not yours to give!
And is the height
A lesser thing
Than is the depth below?
I worship God,
As you shall surely know.'

And each bird rose
In song about Him then.

M. EUANIE TIPPET

Lenten Signs

Here in the city
where impassive pavements
light no signals for seasons,
fingers of woodland
point to the river.

Mottled ivy
wipes off winter dust,
burns greener: a thorn tree
is beginning to sweat
white tears.

Gnarled japonica
bursts into globules of blood,
beading leafless bones;
sunshots dazzle
through crossed boughs

of park lopped trees
and tearing nails of briars.
Robins extemporise
red warnings
of outrageous spring

JOYCE WELDON-SEARLE

Ash Wednesday 1987

Ashes in the snow, death just before the springtime,
Quietly falling, black and white, asleep, side by side
On the passive frozen ground. Sometimes, as you peer,
Cold and anxious, through the late night-frosted window,
You catch a glimpse of a future which isn't there;
A space echoes silently to the solemn sound
Of absent laughter. I have stood too long indoors,
Looking out and seeing what I couldn't believe,
Hoping that there was hope in a hopeless world.
I must go out now, shivering hard in the cold
And in the love and fear, to make the snowmen live,
Using the soft ashes of too many burnt-out fires,
Waiting for the phoenix to arise, painfully,
For each birth will hurt and every joy causes pain,
The sharp sting of sunlight on the tender young shoot
The sheer terror of the fledgling's first soaring flight.
Peace hurts, too, like the cross. I hold on to them both,
Carrying ashes through the snow towards the spring.

TIM NOBLE, SJ

Good Friday at the College, Mirfield

On this Good Friday I started in the light
of Maundy Thursday, dappled with doubt
in the uncertain morn-break, broken bread
and to-be-broken body, then, now, once and always:
Creaking frames and squeaking shoes the silence
gently spoke which strained limbs and aching hearts
gave voice, and must it be? And why me? Can I not
be free from destiny? And can I not go back to
my place at home, to my seat in the nave, to my old employ?
And what is this, such painful abundance of time for what
was once fondly, and with excited haste, done after
work and before cooking the supper?
And how I ache and am sore and want no more
but will try, ask not for whose benefit,
to struggle on here in my unquiet quiet where in the
early light a chillness nudges the blossom and
the bloom and blows clean the still empty tomb.

I sat in the grey light and grey words passed
dimly distant, my praise in defection and rejection
judged and not judged in the vaulted chamber
tested and tried, charges trumped up, emptiness
driving on to seek the full. In garment-tearing
frustration comes the sharp blunt dismissal
and, stupefied by my lack of food, I take my
empty stomach and head on a walk
amazed at flowers and unhinged by birds' wings
who all answered back with the time of year which
claimed life before death, and I understood.
In the budding bursting wood I saw what was
good and my cold ache seemed to thaw in the
gentle greens of praise as my feet went
along the track which led to Calvary.
In the spring-time sun the patient suffering
Passion worked its tortuous course; the cross grew heavy over me,
jarring ever deeper deeper into my flesh and my flesh into
it stumbling on, looking less and less around till only
looking on and up to where it was to stop,
world-stopping, time-stopping, world-timing spot, summit.
And how is the sweat and blood smelt and seen
in our solemn re-enactment of bloodless sweatless
formless forms in youthful shafts of light? And how
am I trembling and panicking in the
slow sureness of movement? And why in the
green brightness outside is the birdsong unreal to my
night? And why onto the grimed sandstone of my sanctuary
does there drip a soul's single shaking tear?

It is finished; it is over. See, there is nothing I
can do, nor give, nor offer but to ask blindly my dull
accusations of him who would a fool of me,
who would a stole on these shrugging shoulders place, who
would his word with these cracked lips proclaim
who would sacraments with these clenched fists dispense
and oil on this cowering head pour which part in wonder
part in worthlessness and part in wilfulness bows.

GEORGE SPENCER

The Cross

The body melts into the cross
like cheese upon a slice of toast,
uproots itself to march across
the world led by the Holy Ghost.

It is a cactus in the spring,
grown in the desert far from sight
where birds may sing of anything
and flowers blossom in the night.

It rages and rampages through
the pages of our history,
an uncontrollable beast, a zoo-
logical mystery.

So much is laid upon its back
it staggers underneath the weight
but not the heaviest blow can crack
its ever-thickening armour-plate.

And yet it's gentle to the touch,
which nobody can understand,
nor why it comforts quite so much
when kissed, or held by human hand.

Some think it thirsty for more blood
and wield it as a sword of war.
Others would bury it in mud:
no value in it any more.

Even evil done in its name
strengthens, does not weaken it.
An instrument of death became
a symbol of the opposite.

MAURICE WEST

The Son's Mother: Good Friday, 1st April

Not in the way of men who tire
Of their loves grown old, did he give
His mother away. Those men conspire
To bury joys, never to relive
In brain a moth memory of their chosen.

Not in the way of a child grown cold
To the trappings of home, did he flee
From his past. That child recasts old
Joys as oppression, in order to free
Moth memory for the new life chosen.

But in the way of one who loses
All to gain, he remembered her virgin loss,
Her youth's joy strewn among lilies and roses;
And straining to wean her from his cross,
Gave her away to the love he had chosen.

Her rose stem has grown, a broken reed
Bruised in the wind and wounded on rood;
Her lithe lily's limbs are draped on rood;
Her live lily now limp, a wind-bruised reed.

SIEW—YUE KILLINGLEY
from *Easter Cycle 1988*

Easter Saturday

'Sleep,' said the voice and I slept.
I trusted the voice and slept.

And a white bird flew out alone
And the white air rolled beneath —
Far below the cliff-top streamed in snow
And dropped away, white bone on bone,
Down to a frozen sea, white wreath on wreath.

And in the secret heart of the bird
From the thin grey desert dawn
Flew the bounding sun that daily
Amazed and spun the cold shift
Of silting sands into gold.

And I saw beneath the frozen sea
The waves live in tumultuous energy.

HEATHER HAWKINS

The Harrowing of Hell

Love asks to penetrate
The hot dark place,
The place of pain,
From which the sons of light
Hide their modest faces.
Love is allowed.
And oh! what gnashing of teeth
Among the demons
Who thought it was their own!

D.M. LEWIS

Easter

The cock crows — a strident omen
piercing the dark and Peter's heart;
daily reminder of his coward's part,
drawing us close, cowards all,
who also shrink from the cup of gall;
heavy-eyed and sadly,
the women, their well of tears now spent,
take up their jars of ointment and spices
and slip out in the sleeping morn. Mary
the wanton follows weeping,

doubting her forgiveness now yet still
longing to atone. To wash His wounded feet
and use her hair again. To hear once more
those sweet words of balm. They come
to the open tomb and find it empty —
empty as a childless womb. Their wonder
and their joy are yet to come. Fears fill
their minds with sense of loss. They run
to tell the others. Slowly the rising sun
wakes the birds to call. The morning mist
shrouds the garden in a chilly veil.
Mary stands lost. Softly as a breath He came
with hands out-stretched to halt her swift embrace.
She knew Him then by the wounded place
in those feet that she had kissed.

M.J. NORMAN

The Stone

Heard in the garden's wakening
the heart's cry 'Where?' the word and meaning
of blade, petal and leaf leaning
to the sun's rising:
of trees' arms thrown to the fair skies,
questioning: graveclothes with care
and neatness folded: and Christ there,
mistaken for the gardener.
But, miracle-moved, burning
in the bright, O the bright, dawning
of the third day's morning
is the stone standing
aside: the live coal briefly held
to the tomb's lips touching their cold
breath to eloquently told
gospels in the morning's gold.

CHRISTOPHER GOODWIN

Easter Sonnet

Dawn breaks in the garden. Flowers unfold
Their petals to the sun. Birds shake their wings
And preen for day. Nocturnal cold
Slowly gives way to warmth. Living things
Drowsily stretch and yawn. A lizard's tongue
Darts at a fly. A busy buzzing bee
Bumbles from bush to bush. Beetles among
The gravel rustle and scurry. Rasping, a key
Turns in the gate. The garden, now awake
Growing and hunting, pauses, holds its breath
Suspended as the mourning women take
Their path towards the tomb to honour death
Stumble, and cry in fear at the first sight
Of the cave's mouth, alive with dazzling light.

BRIGID SOMERSET

Cretan Easter, Saturday Night

We fill the floodlit cathedral square
And listen to the microphoned transmission
Of the Mass that electrifies the air:
'Christ Jesus came to save us who have sinned',
But we heed only local tradition —
Devil's luck if our candles are snuffed by wind.

The approach to midnight heightens tension,
Priestly voices reach a higher pitch,
As the great clock hands reach their ascension
The world goes mad and giant bells ring out
Throughout the city, shooting fireworks stitch
The night with stars and raise the joyful shout:
    'Alethos aneste!' — He has risen indeed!
    As have the winds that blow their ancient creed.

JAMES HARPUR

The Staff of the Kebab House watch the Lighting of the New Fire

From the first spark,
concealed in the rain and the crowd from many,
the gutsy fire bursts up in the new dark

and shows — tucked from the wind
by the cathedral buttress — between stone and brazier
the bishop, his mitre jammmed on, determined.

Christ rises outdoors, anyhow,
to sounds of singing from the Old Mill, sparks
in a light gust flying randomly, now and now.

Indoors back there,
behind plate glass, with folded arms the chefs
in their white overalls stare:

a pageant, an interlude
based on a fire like their own work; ideas
fly in the wind but flames are understood

and they can see how light
bodies itself, complete and visible there,
ready to speak in the rough night.   JENNY KING

Resurrection

When the wind strikes the clock in the hall,
when the rain snipes the latch on the window,
when the snow covers catch and handle and
road and path and grass and Mrs White's car,
when the night stains the TV aerials and trees
with its finger tips, when the parched frost wins
its way down flimsy icicles, and finds
you looking up into the blue winter
wearing only a cold that never ends,
when winter's naked sword is clothed with guile,
the weather its persistent cutting edge,
remember love is often cold and wan
until it finds two voices for its song.
So winter's notes will usher in the spring.   GERALD KELLS

The Flame of Pentecost

A
bit
of a
wisp of
a flame
from the
consuming
purifying
all-blazing
ever-exploding
furnace of love,
our holy Lord God
came down and filled
the Jewish Christians,
enabling and empowering
them to shout His praises
and speak the truth for Him
despite the vested interests
the entrenched bigotry and the
spiritual powers in high places
all fiercely ranged against them
A roaring blast and fiery tongues
came down to shake Jerusalem city
from its normal orthodox smugness
It was the Father's promise given
to His chosen responsive children
expectantly met in adoring prayer
On that unique Pentecost morning
God's Church which must overcome
was begun and equipped with power
and God in the form of His Spirit
succeeded God in the form of His
crucified and ascended Son Jesus
as His Representative on earth
The command still is that we
should be perfect as God is
and continuously be filled
with His own Holy Spirit
and so share His gifts
and obey His leading
and bear His fruit
to the praise of
the triune God
all our days

DUDLEY REEVES

Pentecost

May's got into the morning and made it mad.
Earth's burst, hawthorn's crazy,
air dances on hot bricks, clad
in shimmering leaves, hued with a hazy
idea of going up in fire. Can't see straight.
All bends, twists, comes to bits in the eye.

World's full of winter people, hills full of sky,
veil of visibility's rent.
Nothing is what we knew it by,
everything's what we guessed it meant.
All's new. Ever's better than late!

Shall I weave you another crown
while shoots are soft and thorns are green?
Shall we go dancing round the town,
blue-eyed summer and beauty queen?
Where shall you find your coat of dreams,
weft and warp and with no seams?
Who shall tell you what you mean,
you who stand at Heaven and stare,
where do we go to now from here?

Summer is creeping into things,
land has lift off from the land,
June is coming with golden rings,
smothered in scent and pleasurings.
See and touch my wounded hand,
blessed are those who have not seen!

Each in a little slot of time
groaned for the coming one that went,
grieved for the word that would not rhyme,
dug for the gold already spent,
turned back home and locked the door.

What shall we make of it any more?
Each in a private coat of fear
remembering the things we saw.
Fish for breakfast on the shore!
On the mountain something queer?

Out of water rises wine,
bread in body, air in fire.
First-born of all creation, shine
your shattering into us, break us into one entire
uprising of the dark earth into the Spirit's flame —
the light, the rainbow light of all
things whatever that find in us their truest, brightest
and most lovely name.

PROSPER DOWDEN

Mary Spinning

The running sand hung in the glass;
On the ceiling the dancing water lights
Were suddenly still
And the spindle, flashing on its scarlet thread,
Dropped as her fingers slackened,
The distaff lolling in the crook of her arm
Like an abandoned doll.
Time was suspended and with it all its laws.
The prism gathered up its rainbows
And shone with a white fire.
In the space between two stifled heartbeats
The Holy Spirit like a touch of white-hot steel
Sprang the hardened systems of the world apart,
And when her sluggish blood ran free again
And the ropes of skipping light
Flickered across the fields of red and gold
On her languid eyelids,
The redeeming spark was locked in the meshes of matter.

L.J. ANDERSON
First published in *Christian*

May to Midsummer

May to midsummer is the Holy Ghost's time.
Rhododendron laps the fell foot, lakes
of soft burning; the dark hawthorn in the hedge,
heavy with blood, blossoms
from the solitary and spiny tree.

Composite fire flowers wheel in borders,
multi-coloured the rose buds in the walled garden
and the mauve lightning falls.

Having no image, time and place
conceive; marriage creates
the ascending heat of the sun;
parthenogenesis in flower and space.

The poet juggling his simple symbols
finds them crumbled to dust in his fingers.
This muse is amorphous and will not sleep
in a fancy bed at will, but
breaking image, metaphor and time
is localised in the burning peony and the obedient word.

ALAN SHAW

from Soul Seasons

Earth Life. To furrow my flesh clay,
To sow seed life in lady earth,
To root couch from my soul soil,
To feel full fruit praise:
These grace gifts joy me.

Sunflower. I strain
in ecstasy of nourishing
my ordered world of honeycomb,
these golden seeds in my mighty head.

I struggle too with mighty opposites:
the fulness and sterility
of earth, my careful-careless mother.

I hate to give my golden seeds to death:
my strength is strong to life, not death-to-life.
Yet I am seed of heaven-wed-to-earth
(wild incarnation),
so I must trusting yield my seeds
to earth's dark mothering,
sun's tawny potency.

Autumn Soil.   Autumn soil is rich with much falling,
death of fruit, of seed.

Singing leaf life
spins downwards
to mould new birth.

Sky falls,
dew,
mild mist,
and rain gives grace to the grass.

Willow.   I confess to the ever-virgin willow,
who casts her catkins before her flesh fruits,
what I have tried to do,
what I have failed to do.

Barren tree, I confess
my trying to have,
my striving to do.

I come to you for your womanhood.
Rooted in love-in-death water,
breath dancing through silver-green slivers,
your mothering too deep for present sight.

Virgin willow,
pray for us now.

Sr ELIZABETH REES

Harvest Moon

The swaying aspen glides before our eyes.
Entranced,
           Unaware of snapping twigs,
           Ignoring whipping branches,
We gaze at the orb:
           The hanging harvest moon,
Orange and glowing in an October sky.

Partners in a cosmic dance,
           We creak across hoary grass
As the moon hovers, a fingertip away.

Our steps sing, gravel-throated,
           As we crunch along the moon-lit path,
Wrapped in the frost-scented evening.

A crust of light; the oak door swings:
           We stand inside a cornucopia,
Bearing our muddy potatoes and runner beans.

Lights flicker, spinning out from the cross,
           Glancing off ruddy apples.
Scented sweet-peas overpower, mingling with crumbly earth.

Our voices rise in praise and thanks,
Spiralling upwards,
           To float to the moon.

SIAN MIDGLEY

Autumn

The leaves
Turn again with the year.
God's cold left hand
Wipes out the sun
And the earth is wrapped
In the pale mists of
His hesitation.

Challenged
He indicates two
Drawn close to the hearth
Where apple logs
Crackle in the flame.
A smile passes
Between them and
Her hand is in his.

The angels tremble
As God's great heart
Aches
With love of all this.

ROD KEY

November

      is remembering
         Saints
            Guy Fawkes
              Poppies
                 Leaves falling —
Yet the tree remains
Gaunt and shadowy
In mists
Which gently veil
Some hurts we would forget

Rain falling softly
Through unclothed branches
Becomes a healing
A restoring

So can we accept
Our Novembers —
Our rememberings.

MARY PHILPOT

138

In November

*Ought not these oldest sufferings of ours to be bearing more
fruit by now?* (Rilke)

November searches me.
When thrushes sing requiem
in the yellow chapel of elm and lime
and starlings try old texts,
how I long for a steady rhythm,
the sweet iambics of amended life.

To be orderly and convinced!
To have stored a single unblemished fruit!
On the table a basket
of smutted pears; outside,
ladder not stowed away,
secateurs lost and barrow piled
with nameless soft corruptions.

In a house of twigs a child weeping
for the pattern the kaleidoscope
will not give back. Against a stone
dahlias in a jar. In Arden
an old fool particoloured
venting his observation
in mangled forms.

Was it always too late?
Seventy times seven, seventy times seven
sang a voice in the fallen garden
but labouring Adam never turned to ask
for a second chance.

M.R. PEACOCKE

Two Christmas Haiku

Candles on a tree
Bring light to dark December
And warmth to cold hearts.

In the bare branches
No birds sing, but in the sky
Shines a Christmas star.

VERA ROBERTS

An Advent Tree

It is ridiculous
That this small tree
Is spinning like a meteorite
In Sainsbury's car-park.

Lit by a gaudy streetlight,
Its dwindling leaves hang
By their golden fingertips
Twirling fire.

Christ's birth too
Caught men by surprise,
Raw with glory
On a winter night.

THELMA FISHER
First published in *Christian*

Mother

When that child was born, did He enter
this world meekly?
Or was He pushed, midst screams, protesting
from the haven of His mother's womb?
Did the triumphant agony of her labour
conceal an ecstasy of death?
Did she know then?

And when the shepherds came to marvel,
Those men of earthly toil and commonsense,
Could they foresee the ebb within the flow?
And did she know?

H. LENNON

And
the
lostness
of
a
snuffed
candle
marks
an end
of
Christmas
a birthday cake
a power cut
an experiment
on oxygen or time
a church service
a special space
for meditation
a meal
a day
a prayer

yet in the heaped wax at its
base
a story finds Once upon a time.

DAPHNE CRAIG

Christmas Poem

Yes baby, well may you cry
— the trouble you've caused.
Love of drama on somebody's part is responsible
for the tragedy and pathos, contradiction and paradox.
A father who isn't your father,
A mother without a husband,
soon to lose her son, but not so soon
as others who knew nothing of your birth,
who went obediently forth and multiplied
only to lose their own because you have been born.
You, christened 'God with us'
                              mighty God of all power
supposedly anthropomorphized by a feeble, dirty
son of much-maligned-by-gossip mother,
not even refugeed, just come too late
to where, but for others, there would have been room.
You, nick-named 'Love', born without the love-act
of parents who, it seems, had not embraced
full physical joys of consummated love.
You're not the first to feel the pangs
of being born.
Others have more to cry about
but weaker lungs to make their misery known.
No bombs threaten you, no starvation
wrinkles your mother's breast and makes her nipple
pale, useless, uncomforting, a dehydrated pea.
Straw's quite warm, compared with nothing,
whatever 'swaddling bands' may be
or how friendly the animals feel
to the wailing intruder.
The stable, an unfortunate necessity for a day or two,
later to be cherished as romantic dreams of youth
by a comfortable mother in a Nazareth home.
However abnormal your family, they care for each other,
giving you security and human love.
You feel no crippling pains, nor even have
a shameful handicap to cry about.
For thirty years, all that a man may want is yours.

Why is it, then, that in your cry I hear
the misery of the world?
and in your eyes I see
comprehension and forgiveness of everything
including me?
Why is it in your birth it seems
everyone is born?
and in your utter helplessness
God's strength is shown?

Unhappy baby, do not cry for me.
Maturity will bring the need to die for me,
so save your tears.
Choke your breath in the straw,
to escape the death of living
knowing all.
Harden your heart, to avoid the open wounds of feeling
all, for all.
Leave it to another to be God's son,
Go back and suggest to Him it's too much for one
man to bear. Beg Him to share
the burden between all babies
past, present and to come.
Then return, and just cry for your milk.

ALWYN MARRIAGE
from *Beautiful Man*

Christmas Night

Sacred, sombre, silent night.
Stars unstill in fierce assertion
Seize the sky. The moon steers
A sickle sail through clouds of muslin light.
I study
The cold air chilled on the spiked white ground
From morning's nativity.

A spear of sorrow Jack-frost piercing
In sharp iced steel.
'Simeon, Simeon.'
I stagger
Uneasy
With the stare of stars.

Rejoice! Rejoice!
The carolling sky of Sirius,
Blue with an acid that touches off pure flame,
Revolves declarant constellations
And there
The high bright star in its sure place
Pouring down rimed roof-tops cascades of praise.

E. J. MATYJASZEK

The Christmas Child

He lies behind a snuffed-out star
Half-suffocated by our tinsel lies
We leave Him in a manger in the outer dark
And when in spring He runs to us
And begs us day on day to open wide our eyes
We wind our warped, sham love to thorn
And crucify the Christmas Child.

KENNETH C. STEVEN

Good Shepherd

Yes, I was there the night the heavens rang
with angel song and dazzled us below.
I heard each syllable the spirits sang,

and, yes, I heard them order us to go.
If I had gone, who would have watched the flock?
My favourite ewe was lame and pregnant, so

I had no wish to leave her. And the stock
is valuable. What if thieves should find
our beasts? I waited, heard the morning cock

crow distant sunrise. All at once my mind
swarmed with portentous murmurings of deep
betrayal. Was I wrong to stay behind?

No minute of that night was spent in sleep.
Good shepherd. I would die to save my sheep.

ALISON CHISHOLM

Christmas Day: North Wales, 1987

The colour of the day was that of slate
out of the sun's eye. I peered
into hedges and scanned fields
for signs of the Nativity remembering
how as a child I could always
spot the star. Only a poplar tree
for a moment became the shape
of an angel's wing, at least what I thought
an angel's wing ought to be like.
Other signs there were none:
no Mary-blue sky; no sweet smell
of blossom to hover like frankincense;
not even a Herod-wind flailing in the branches.
God fails with the spectacular.
We do not want His ordinariness
more than our own, Our minds
will always demand more than a Bethlehem and stable shit.

ALED JONES-WILLIAMS
First published in *Christian*

Christmas!
Once
Advent's adventure
Pregnant with hope.
Now
A cradle empty
Aching for mystery;
A candle-gutted
Cruciform darkness
Lit by a winsome Love
Heralding Easter.

ROGER HAYDEN

The Birth

Take fright this night
For strangeness' sake,
Or glory in the tumult — Shout!
For all agree
'Tis small, and aching sweet,
This Boy-king, gravely bundled.

We saw him after the angels came
(as if the stars had dropped to treetop height,
And sung for honesty and awe)
He saw us, too, unblinking, calm,
In majesty.

We found out later what it cost:
All wealth in this and worlds beyond,
All wisdom deep and wide,
No weapons, only Love itself,
And the pain in Mary's side,
Allowed, as all his pain would be,
For Thee.

THOMAS TURNBULL

In the Beginning

The choir comes for Christmas,
A contained world, already created
From separate elements, mainly
Small boys

Settling like winter locusts
Under the mistletoe-bedecked lamp,
Grasping oranges from the art deco bowl
With greedy fingers; expertly demolishing

Building blocks of cake, blackly rich
With Corinthian fruit, pilasters of almond,
Architraves of icing. Reducing sweet creation
To crumbs.

In unison, the sweet
Singing rises
To the high ceiling,
Telling of ivy and holly,

Deer running through greenwood,
Wassail cup of rosemary tree,
Obliterating marvellously
The significance of the night.

Offers only brightness
In the icons of faces,
Burnished, untarnished, eager
To hurry away, start out,

Satisfied to map the dark
With their newly-won moons of silver,
Confident of hailing
Another smiling morn.

CAROLE ROBERTSON

Extracts from *Epiphany*: a fourteen-part journey

I.   Who were they, the men poised between reality and myth?
     Kings? Wise men? Strangers from a faraway land?
     Did they breathe stardust, leave it lying around
     for us to breathe again? Were they aware
     of their existence, question the notion
     of a transcendent deity? If they perceived,
     through the unfortunate coincidence of being wise,
     the magnitude of their revelation, did they immediately
     slip from the confines of the temporal
     into the liberty of infinity?

               O Come, Come,
               Come King Emmanuel,
               Don't want this Jesus-baby
               wrapped up in tinsel;
               but the crystallized moments
               of heaven on earth,
               the stillness, the crying,
               the silent shriek
               of Adam's consummation.

X.   But still we do not know
     where they were coming from
     or where they went when they
     returned by another way
     (Show me the way).
     We only know that they brought gifts,
     symbols of our own life and experience.
     I do not think such perfect symbols
     had extension, took up space within
     the real stable, or when God accepted them
     there was a change in the visual field
     of Jesus.

     No gift can be brought to the world's source:
     at best we can seek through metaphor
     for the offering-up of intense experience
     before the ultimate.
     The slow and steady steps approach no throne;
     the culmination of the world's deep wisdom
     bows before the unknown.

XI.   We do not know where they were coming from,
    but we must learn to lose and still to love,
    to love yet willingly let go.

> Myrrh-man murmuring
> of sin to the innocent
> sadness to the singers, doom
> as from the womb spring
> king and baby.

We do not know their route, what country they passed
    through,
yet find that faith holds us despite ourselves,
when all else is rejected, will not go.

> Mystical moment in
> movement of frankincense,
> seared in the fire, till frank, intense
> white heat of purity
> kindled of Incarnation.

We cannot guess what lay ahead of them when they had seen
the light:
we weep despairingly when the hope we live by seems deception,
but still accept its guidance for our life.

> Gold, from one too old
> to covet, to one too young to care.
> Cold is the glow of gold
> Child beside your fire.

ALWYN MARRIAGE
from *Beautiful Man*

Her Dream at Christmas

She went back to church after years
— not penitent, rather curious
about how things had altered there —
but she wasn't prepared for this.

In place of the old-style communion,
when thin priests would grimly spare
a dry biscuit, and a sniff of wine
was all the drink they'd ever share

. . . instead of that, she saw this:
there was nut-loaf on the choir stall,
with each prayer-book a banana split.
There was quiche, crab salad, lemon fool.

There on the font sat a turkey roast,
parsnips, carrots, sprouts spilled over.
The whole church was a perfect feast!
On the pews stood raspberry pavlova.

And where the faithful knelt in line
drinks were unsteadily dispensed
from a box of chilled Italian wine.
She knew the price must be immense.

She fled back home and found a place
of hunger — rooms of emptiness.
Then she fell asleep for forty days
and woke with this need to confess.

MARTYN CRUCEFIX

Experience of God

Dialogue   (Between the Soul and its Creator)

I am the clown, the jester, the strumpet,
the tart with the heart
made of gold.

You are play-acting, concealing your crying,
The room of your womb
hurt and cold.

I am the sinner, the wayside-faller,
easy-rider,
back-slider.

You are high-flying, gliding,
soaring sky-higher
cloud-niner.

I am the betrayer, the coward, the deceiver,
trapped in the web
of my laugh.

You are my prize, my joy and my partner,
caught on the cross of my love.

Mary's Song 3

You can swallow your wine at a gulp,
or make it last for an evening.
You can be busy with your body
and empty in your mind.

It is easier to feed a hungry man
than to satisfy your soul.
Easier to fill your days with busy nothings,
than to recognize your need.

Easy, it is easy to eke out your perfume
day by day,
and let the wind snatch the smell into nothing.
Easier still to keep the stopper in the jar
all your life.

It is easy to make people angry
by being yourself;
by smashing the jar.

Yet I have anointed my beloved,
I have touched his skin with my hair
and his soul with my soul.
I have filled a house with fragrance.

I have lived for an hour.
The fragrance lingers for ever.

ELAINE MILLER
First published in *Christian*

Judgment

For I the Lord your God am an unjust God,
And fling my unfairness like a thick warm cloak
Over the cold hard naked bones of justice,
So that even in her hands you lie soft and safe:

For what do you know of justice, small one,
With your demands for fairness? Two equals two,
Love equals joy, injury requital?
But justice is far different from that.

MY justice is the FIAT of creation,
But fallen creatures are too weak to bear it,
And in my love I smile in myriad judgments.
The Judgment of the rain issues in apple blossom
And a thousand more flowers; of the wind issues
In seedling forests; of ripe grain in bread,
And bread in music, and music in My praise.
O small and dear, rest in my unfairness
Whose name is mercy, and learn to reap
What you have not sown, and not to reap
What you have sown; and bless My grace
That you are spared the reaping.

MARGARET MOFFAT BROWN

The Perfect Number

Outside in the garden,
old-fashioned leaves fall from a queer tree.
Stuff grows in sudden, beneficent clumps
and the pleasure of dwelling on things is endless.

Somewhere in the universe
a lesion splits the skull and out steps Christ
like an obscure and beautiful equation:
the Perfect Number.

MICHAEL CULLUP

Contemplation

I saw Him in the crushed crimson's dawn appearing
banner-flung across the Eastern sky.
In mute-misery for lack of vision
lost-longing gathered to a sigh.
I could not hold brazen beauty's
fleet, faint, fragile cobweb of design
I cried for the far-flung Godhead
grasping, grappling to make the beauty mine.
Dare not scan the crowned Redeemer hanging
lashed, gashed fast upon the tree
garment-dyed Jesus, stripped and naked
blood poured forth because of me.
On wind's winged chariot, He comes riding
Stallion-drawn, whirl-wheeled, fleet
sword-buckled King, re-armed in glory
I fall, love adoring at his feet.

JEAN NAYLOR

The Ark

Be thankful
he didn't build it in the cellar
where the vision
which became a boat
could not be sneered at.

Noah would have felt
a right twit
struggling to launch an ark
full of elephants and fleas
and the other paraphernalia
of creation
from the basement.

His hope was built
for all to see
and jeer at.
Nails, wood, ladders,
pots of pitch, brushes,
the clobber
of a boat-builder
preparing to float.

In the open
God flings his promise
across the sky
shouts
'I love you'
in the spangled curve
of sun through rain
which holds the earth
with a striped handle.

FELICITY PRESCOTT
First published in *Christian*

Scarecrow

He stands, guarding his field.
No Priapus this, of monstrous
Sexuality.
No:
Sexless, ageless, he stretches forth
His wooden arms
In mindless sacrifice
And in un-good, unspoken
Benediction
Blesses the field.

But look, closer:
Those wooden arms, that one stout leg
Are not the whole.

Through the torn sleeve-ends see
The soon-to-be-carrion flesh,
Hands cupped and clawed
Round the restricting nails.
Behind the turnip-face another, registering
All pain the world has ever known
Or will.
Under the crude hat the blackthorn rips
Into the tender flesh, and where
The two feet share
The one nail, transfixing them
To the one stump, the blood drips down
Onto the fertile field.

Forsaken, alone,
The fading figure
Does not call down
Deserved damnation
Upon the perpetrator
Who farms the land,
Permits this dumb charade,
But suffers
This lonely vigil
Simply to scare away
A few black crows,
So that the field might flourish
The crop
Surpass all expectations.

PAM GIDNEY
First published in *Envoi 80*

Ichthus

Belief is commoner than before. Now
Leaves on the tree are falling in
Autumn's sunlight as on the goldilocks of
Christ. The Jew was (you may have read)
King and fished in all the filthiest canals.

J.P. WARD

I Sing a New Christ

I sing a new Christ, the joyful, merry guest,
Who fills with wine your empty cup,
Listens when song is your heart's pursuit,
He blesses the wedding, and its fruit,
All the children as they grow up.

I sing a new Christ, the hero of weekdays,
His halo of fine wood-fire spun
The one who from workshops builds a church
From cotters' laments makes psalms emerge
The Carpenter, the people's son.

I sing a new Christ, terror of profiteers
His whip will bring wonders diffused
Who out of oppressed millions' sorrow
Will conjure a new Earth tomorrow
The Christ of the crushed and the abused.

Come, let us open wide like a mouldy barn
Christ's church that was almost a jail
Scatter the seeds and spread his new Word
Till in all the sad hearts it is heard
In factory, meadow, hill and dale.

TIBOR TOLLAS
Translated from Hungarian by Livia Varju

The Way

If not for
slap of trainers on tarmac
one might as well be
centuries back
in pre-industrial
pre-Raphaelite time.

So dark, but for
stars unseen through haze
of city light, spreading
uncountable, even the Plough
once tracked then lost
for years, spotted again.

Only a torch
startles crickets,
keeps to the road.

                        At such times
God wanders through the woods
like some wild animal,

and a kind of fear
treads the darkness
like a high-wire artiste
counting each step

not seeing the line's end,
repeating
               nearly there
               nearly there

STEPHEN WALING
First published in *Christian*

Red Poppy
Translated by author from his original Welsh

Is this the religion of comfort,
with the sower,
gathering the stones
and clearing the brambles and the thorns,
having to bleed
for his pains?

But on the breeze
his wounds released
a song
from the ridge on the edge of the field,
like the red poppy in the wheat,
and called it another comforter.

EUROS BOWEN
First published in *Christian*

Cross Consciousness

'I am the wound in the sky
Through which the sun interminably pours;
You by my pain, I by yours
Illumined; and the shadows lie
Across the earth, arrayed
In vast crossed bands of light and shade.'

You are the wound in my side
O God, you teach me how to move
In pain and how to prove
Your love. My power denied
And the contours of the world defined
By the shadows of a troubled mind

In the form of a cross. (The round
Earth dissected into four, in a flood
Of light, running in sweat and blood
In the path of the sun.) A crown
Of light pierces the world. The singing fire
In me will never be expired.

Used to you now; the simple print
Of you on me can never be removed.
Mark out your presence in the still grooves
And valleys of my heart; places extinct
Except for you. Sensing you displaces,
I feel you move me into wider spaces.
My lips purpling with your kiss
As the long cross sheds its shadow on the green.
Light shivering on the lawn, rising unseen
While I remain here, impaled by a wish
To become more; to see if, by what you gave
We both could rise together from one grave.

OLIVIA MICHAEL
First published in *Christian*

Seeing

She says, at three she saw God.
Strip eighty years: pinafored,
Button-booted, she's alone,
Tottering down a back lane
To the corner shop, proud of being
Trusted to run an errand, seeing

No-one about. Suddenly
This man comes towards her, he
Walks strangely, seeming to skim
The cinder path. She knows him
Instantly and turns, heads terrified
For home where safety is: those inside

Laughed at her tale and we now
Who hear can't help thinking how
Simple the old get, senile
Even, so with nod and smile
Steer the talk round to the commonplace,
Yet can't ignore that look her old face

Wears, a total credence, calm
Certainty. Belief's a flame
That someone, something, once lit
In childhood and burns still. It
Isn't terror but the otherness
Stumbled into then, growing no less,

Has marked her: this being sure,
Though housebound, old and poor,
Arrests the twinge of pity.
Look in her face and envy.
God walks back lanes, angels perch in trees.
Sometimes, rarely, someone looks and sees.

SYBIL BIRCH
from *The Single Mind* 1980

A Question of Wood

He who grew up
    with wood around
    ran with infant feet on sawdust ground
    who in childhood played
    with wooden toys made by a caring father
    yet with youthful hand
    learnt to whittle wood
    shaping pieces to his own command.

What dreadful irony
decreed that wood should be
his instrument of death
and could it be
that Joseph once embraced
that traitor tree?

At the very end
did wood become his enemy or friend?
Did splinters stab his arms
when outstretched
for the nailing of his palms?
Or did dear familiarity
carve comfort even then
evoking honest kindly men
ladles or the mother's chair
and a working carpenter?

PEGGY POOLE
First published by Headland Publications

The Uninvited Guest

He seems to come in like the leaves —
Blown in at the open window,
And always on a light and airy day,
Never in stormy weather.
And always, I've noticed,
At an inconvenient time —
Right in the middle of the washing.
He looks at me and shows me these holes in his hands,
And, well, I can see them in his feet.
'Not again,' I say,
'Please don't stand there bleeding
All over the kitchen floor.'

Sometimes he comes softly, sadly,
At night — close, by the side of my bed —
Sometimes I latch the door —

But he never goes away.

THELMA LAYCOCK

O Taste and See . . .

I opened my eyes.
In the dark a baby crying . . . my child demanding milk.
I picked her up, soothed her, put her to my breast.
Her milky smiles showed her contentment, and the room
     (save for her snuffling, suckling joy-soaked self)
        Was silent.

My thoughts turned to God . . . I craved His caress.
The silence was almost tangible, and peace flowed through the
     room.
I lay there still and quiet, enjoying His presence;
     blissful, I drank of His sweetness until, like my baby,
       I slept.

GILL ASHTON

In All Points

He runs brown fingers over silken wood,
The knots showing dark like nipples
In the grain. Bread-smells everywhere
And ripe soft fruits to burst against the teeth.

We had leaflets on Careers
And talks from counsellors and students.
We thought we chose, although we later knew
What gentle things a frown, a word, can do.

Jesus stands and wipes his sweaty hands
Over his apron in the burning noon:
A life like other lives, scaled down to this —
Chisel, shavings, nails and the cheapened kiss.

ANDREA MITCHELL
First published in Christian

A Man Alone

There are fuller powers than we had earlier known
when the muscled leap declared our adulthood,
when debate was a gauntlet thrown,
caught up, then tossed in our triumphant mood.

Searching latterly through the patient years' scope
we see a man, thrust upward by a high endeavour,
carve a design where massive strength dare not hope
to climb, gain peaks impregnable to the clever.

Eyes clear, careful, we see a man alone, against the sky,
sending rare words upon the air with quiet breath;

see how the learned and fierce choose him to crucify
while he at last frees them, and all, from death

For ever!

A.L. HENDRIKS

Holding Hands with God

Having a hand,
having nothing better to do with it,
she gave it God to hold.
You might as well take it, she said,
no one else wants it.

Tried not to sound bittter,
tried to feel generous and loving,
waited with some apprehension,
wondering sometimes
what she did it for.
It didn't feel safe
and wasn't what she'd call erotic.

Best was when they sat quiet and still
and she could feel just ordinary.
But when that thumb caressed
the inside of her wrist,
she got the shivers;
found herself this end
of a shaky wooden footbridge,
nothingness below, the other side
pitch dark for ever and ever.
Did she have to cross it?

She tried remonstrating.
Don't push so hard, she'd say.
What do you want?
I do my bit, don't I,
go to church, read the lesson,
make cakes, help at the fête,
stand up and get myself counted?
Can't we leave it at that?
And that's not all:
there's the PCC,
the other committees,
the magazine,
the Deanery.
What else must I do?
Put in for the Papacy?
Sing hymns in Woolworths stark naked?
You weren't my first choice, you know,
so don't get above yourself:
I'll do it my way in my time;
just practise patience.

And God went on stroking
and wanting.

ANN DEUTSCH

Briefing

He will be an affable man — surprising you
With the warmth of his handshake. Only when
He smiles, you may notice something about his eyes:
Not squinting, exactly — more a sort of nibbling —
A quality of focus.
                    You will walk,
Slowly at first, along the orchard rows,
While he picks fruit — handing you pears and peaches
(Beautiful, perfect things you do not eat);
And he will talk such sweetness, his words curling
In tendrils, curious and delicate,
(Sometimes touching your arm to emphasize
Or reassure) until, of a moment,
He will fall silent, and your pace will quicken
(The orchards dropping behind you now, the path
Grown stony, thin birds hanging in the air,
The sun an egg of fire, your pockets heavy
With untouched fruit, and him, still saying nothing);
And what with the sun, the rancour of your feet,
The silence of this man, his peeled-grape eyes,
His double-breasted suit and the dark thirst
That scratches at your throat, you will grow mad —
Your fingers catching at his face for words
Or water, while the bright fruit in your pockets
Glows and the ripeness of his smile says, 'Eat'.

ROBERT CARVER

Jesus in the Wilderness

Hungry, He prays at night,
outstaring stone after stone
preparing to cry out;

not changing them into bread
but hearing promises, promises
whispered in His light head.

FRED SEDGWICK

Letter to Proctor

It was night
And the sky became a great stillness
Pale without stars
I saw the wind turn with love
Sighing in the trees —
Rain and darkness were one
In the stillness of quiet
The sky sank back upon the earth
Then every flower broke open — spilled —
The wind blew out its water into darkness
— I breathed
And in the silence — heard the sweetness of the rose.

SUE ARENGO
First published in *Acumen* 1989

Parable 41

What human love in its utmost passion
can rival the Goddess smoothing damp hair
of a worshipper after he has worked
through the swelterings of vineyard for Her?

Could a father give daughters stones to eat?
Even so, heavenly Mother will not.

Could a woman abort the child she feels?
Even so, heavenly Father will not.

Jesus, not Paul, revealed the Trinity.

THOMAS KRETZ

On Being a Christian

Agnosticism

It doesn't come easy.

In spite of it all,
I can't help pushing open
the doors of country churches;
shoving a coin or two
in the box on the wall,
paying twice over
for the leaflet I take.

It doesn't come easy.

Wandering among gravestones
is irresistible;
departure is almost
impossible. I delay
it over and over
to hear once more the song of the blackbird.

It doesn't come easy.

As I race back
into the modern
rationalistic world,
I think of cathedral towns
and country rectories
and gentle rectors' wives
arranging the flowers.

JOHN TATUM

Faith

Suddenly
the fear
huddles
in my belly

My vision,
ripped, hangs
about me
like a shroud.

Try to remember
the triumphant
banner I wore
yesterday

billowing sure
in the courage and light
but feel like
the voyeur

of someone else's
half-forgotten dream.
Here at the edge, hoping I won't

retreat, scared
I can't go on,
I stand
eyes shy praying

Jesus Jesus.

Hands

My hand lying with yours
flat on the full heavy curve
of your warm belly, we embrace
in our bed's intimate darkness
listening, almost, for the sudden
jabs of movement within.
Fearful wonder at this miracle
draws our hands together in prayer
to the Father who blesses us daily.

LIAM BLACK

Image II

Women, who
would take the freedom trail,
must make a long
journey to the interior.

Many were the dry years
of the Exodus,
and we, too, travel-weary
sometimes question why
we took the path
                    into the wilderness

Though our shoes pinched before
at least we knew the contours,
walked accordingly.
Now all is new — barefoot
we clench our toes
against the burning sand.

We are the history
we journey through,
for we have taken in
the world outside
and been re-formed, de-formed,
shaped in a man-made mould.

The journey into freedom has to be
self seeking, as we break
new ground in a familiar landscape,
go to meet the challenge,
know and show God in our midst
                    — hidden in the desert rock
which we must strike
to compel forth
that living water, water of dispute
without which
there's no arriving
                    in the Promised Land.

BRIDGET ANN WALKER

A Requirement

And it is required
    that I should be as a shard:
    but breaking is a costly thing.

Mary broke alabaster
    for the outpouring of spikenard
    and the fragrance that filled the house
    was her delight.

It is by breaking the old
    that the Potter fashions the new:
    He pours His Spirit for our wholeness
    and His delight.
And it is required
    that I should be as a shard —
    surely this shall be my delight.

FELICITY YOUNG

Denominations

'Religion, dear?' she asked,
Consent Form held
Below her sterile smile.
'Christian,' I answered.
(One can always hope.)
'It means WHAT DENOMINATION, dear,'
She said.
'Christian,' I tried again,
Lying in silly bath cap, baby's gown,
Awaiting my Pre-Med.
She thought me simple in the head.
'No, no. That isn't what it means.
What Church do you attend?
I need it for my file.'
'CHRISTIAN,' I bellowed,
Cross, unchristianlike.
'I'll worship God in any church:
It's all the same to Him,
If not to us.'

She said I mustn't make a fuss;
They had to know which minister
To call, in case I died.
Such words of comfort!
'Let them all come and save my soul.
I'll need their prayers
If I am dead.
Religion isn't rationed yet,' I said.
'They'd want to know about the burial,'
She answered, sharper now,
Thinking me frivolous.
'We meet all sorts!'
eyes rolled towards her friend.
A needle brought our conversation
To an end.
I had no time to pray.
'Oh put her down as C of E'
I heard the Sister say.

MARY SHEEPSHANKS

Epithalamial Sonnet

For I saw very surely that our substance is in God, and I also saw that God is in our sensuality . . . (Mother Julian of Norwich)

Come tender-free, soft naked to our bed, my gentle dove;
no clothen garb gap-making 'twixt myself and thee.
Then together shall our entwined limbs our constancy
and, in full healing clasp, our oneness prove.

Leave the lamp burning, so that we — mouths enwov-
en, each from other nothing hiding, flesh as we be,
yet faith-keeping, true-trust-telling — open-ey'd shall see
each other down-stripped, yet Christ-transfigured by our love.

Taking-taken and tender; eager caressing-playful feet; bold-
ly and softly, our heart-mind-soul barriers drop. Heart warms,
so each-other-enfolded, thus are we opened to enfold,
sinking closer together in fullness, fallen-heavy in each other's arms.
Solemn and ridiculous, we, new Adam's son and daughter,
are made one by sensuality — and Heaven's laughter!

ROY AKERMAN

Knowing Nothing

I find myself
uncertain, unsure.
Perhaps this is
reason to trust.

I feel like
the dancers caught out
at the disco, as the record
is suddenly cut,
                              mid beat
so we can laugh at
fools with legs half-raised,
arms waving in the air.

I am left knowing nothing,
wondering where to go,
and staying at the crossroads,
stuck in the middle of Your world.

RUPERT LOYDELL
First published in *Christian*

Nihil Obstat

There can be no impediment to grace —
Unless it be the sharpness of the way,
The priestly pride and passions of the race,
The enmities that human throngs obey,
The hardness of the heart, the sullen walls,
The Temple's holies banning alien folk
Where zealotry in righteous anger calls
To rid the holy ground of Caesar's yoke.

Should these deter the enterprise that takes
Its measure from their cause, intimidate
The love that in their very depth remakes
The peace, retrieves the truth, they violate?
Emmanuel the Christ is born, *nihil obstat*
In earth or hell. Let Mary sing *Magnificat*.

KENNETH CRAGG

The Vine

All my fruit is yours for you are mine,
The root and stem from which my tendrils twine;
You are the warmth that swells my tender grapes.

My leaves are hands uplifted to your light;
Each palm grows bright to catch the falling sun,
And when the waiting nets of night
Are wide to hold earth's ripeness we are one —
Root, branch, and leaf and rounding fruit begun
In life's full circle.
White root, go deep
That in your tunnelled darkness I may sleep;
Strong branch, reach high
Till my green hands, glad servers of the sun,
Receive the cup of water and of fire
And find it brimmed with wine —
I drink you drain you till my life in yours
Is yours in mine.

PHOEBE HESKETH
First published in *Christian*

Still, Like a Child

Like a child
still in the womb
I pray, my knees bent
and my head bowed.

Like a child
still in the womb
I wait, trembling at the largeness
of the world
into whose incomprehensible hands

You will deliver me.

ANDREW M. RUDD

Firewood

If it is you that I want
what you ask
is that I become
as driftwood
washed up
upon your shore
to be

> bleached by the sun
> pounded by the surf
> scoured by the sand

until I,
hollowed hallowed
dry and brittle
am ready
for the spark

> which ignites

for the fire

> which consumes

for the smoke

> which sanctifies.

I burn fiercely
leaving only
ash
warm sand
and the taste of salt.

CRAIG STEELAND

Evensong: (for Harriet)

Sky is rolling up its metal.
It is hot at the edges,
glowing and split,
disclosing an arctic vacuum.
Trees on the ridge are breathless,
suddenly bone and joint,
while down here the valley smokes,
half slumped in darkness.
Air, dank as stone.
We wait, until night spans
like the vault of a church.

CHRIS DUNKERLEY

A Tenuous Joy

I walk on air,
Cloud-stepping Heaven's shining span —
And yet with care
Lest all my dreams should vanish in
Despair.

When shall I know
The substance of these fragile hopes
Which ebb and flow,
Yet lure me on forever with
Their glow?

Oh — hold me fast
In all my giddy skyward ways,
That first and last
Your touch will prove my vertigo
Has passed!

Then calm and still
My joy shall be, not tenuous
But waiting, till
These wavering flights of mine fulfil
Your will.

MARGARET CONNOR

A *Thought on the Sinking of the* Herald of Free Enterprise

We take our touch
Around the glimpse of life,
Refusing disbelief in pain
And what the gods are tumbling
Through the agony of man.

We take our touch,
Meeting a gravity
That will never greet the sun again
With a gathering laughter.

For a grief worse than our own
Has turned the mirror of our hearts
Into a mirror of stone.

For the hard of another's grieving
Has lengthened our own pain
Into a dark-browed tenderness,
Into a lengthening love,
That only the teardrops of God
Can lengthen into laughter again.

Yes
I Am the teardrop of God,
I Am the broken dark,
The Light in the broken heart,

The Watcher by the rim of pain.

PETER MORRIS

I AM

I have been blind
so I know what it is to see.
I have been a prisoner in myself
as I watched the lilies growing easily
beside still waters.

I have struggled to write psalms
and understand divinity
praying out loud in a temple
where the crowd sold trinkets.
I am a Pharisee.

Help me to know who I am
for I AM is eternity.

SUSIE MYERS

God's House

Our pew was halfway back; father sat
when he'd given out *Sankey's Sacred Songs*
(we didn't stare at late-comers).

There was a children's bit — once a Welshman
told Bunyan's *Holy War* in seventeen parts —
then pastor prayed for backsliders.

Each month believers were baptized;
schoolgirls sat in the gallery to watch.
Pastor pushed people under, then pleaded for more.

T.E. DOWLEY

Praise and Prayer

Psalm 151

I am come, a long time after the event, to say that *God is Here;*
and not merely in the candlelit places, nor the souls of the inspired,
but in this street.
He is running like the winter, like the rain along this street.
He is dancing with the leaves in the gutter.
He is in the music of the elderly tramp, blowing and gasping on the
wet and windy corner. He is in the bobbing masses moving
unconsciously to the rhythm of the music.
He is trembling with the trees, with the sky mirrored in the shop
window; he is entwined around the railings of the yard where scrap
is sold.
He is hidden in the averted faces of the crowds as they shuffle
along the street with downturned vision. He is the new grass
parting the concrete, and the artistry of a snail.
Oh the Lord is in me and may not be measured. Within the convoluted
folds of this raincoat, I am extended inwards to all infinity.
In the wet blue darkness the car lamps shine, and are captured by
the myriad drops of rain, and the running streams of water on the
pavement.
Each lamp reflects the light of the sun, and is in turn reflected
by the shop windows, which are reflected in other shop windows,
and so on world without end.
So the Lord makes his face to shine upon me, and leads me to the
places of light.
Glory be to the stars, and to the beetles, and to his holy substance;
Which, as it was in the beginning, is now and ever shall be.

OLIVIA MICHAEL

The Complete Works of St Augustine

So many lies!
Then love comes true.
You made us for yourself, Oh Lord,
And our hearts are restless
Till they rest in you.

JOSEPH EVANS

Prayer

1.   i do not kneel,
    not, I hope, because
    i am a proud man
    but for the fear of
    pride, and the
    dark glamour of
    outward signs.

    besides humans are
    always on their knees
    before God.
    especially when
    standing.

2.   if i chant a poem,
    and the audience
    suddenly realise
    it is they
    not i who wrote it
    then i'm praying

    when i take my
    place on the
    picket line and
    someone gobs
    into my face

    and i look up
    and see
    not an enemy
    but a different kind
    of victim
    then i'm praying . . .

    let my voice
    be a cobblestone
    smashing
    against a
    riot shield.

BILL LEWIS
from *Rage Without Anger*

Contemplation

Come dark, come daylight; and the longest hour,
From Mattins bell which signalled my resolve
Until the tower clock should signal my release,
Ate rust and iron into my very soul.

My feet were fastened in the stocks of prayer;
An hour-long thrash for shreds of recollection,
Year-in, year-out. The memory of it mocked
My scrambled silences, invited to despair.

So time passed into timelessness, how many years?
From Mattins till the clock struck off my chains
A trackless desert, dry, too parched for tears,

Till I acclimatised to that accursed land
And met my Lord there. Meeting quite absurd;
We nodded, smiled, and passed without a word!

ANTHONY DUNCAN

Praise

For misty gossamers
— those early strings of silver
woven blade of leaf to blade,
for all commonplace country things
—the anguished prayer
of thorns, the blaze of berries
and the last fiery leaf of the year
floating in blue air
— I give praise.

And praise, too,
for these dark trees drawn against
the last smoke of the day,
for the steaming frosty earth
burning in the sure slow flame
of birth and decay;
for the first owl to fly
and the earliest star to hatch
in the faded chaos
of the western sky.

And so — to be one,
quiet and sure, with these
that so speak what they are,
web, thorn and berry,
earth, owl, tree and star;
to know them
the living stuff, the weave
of the one and only miracle
we call God
— for now,
is prayer enough.

JOHN PULLING

In St Cuthbert's Shrine, Durham

I have sent bright names,
the coins of prayer,
over the saint's stone
in search of blessing.
One of them is yours.
There on the smooth rock
it spins in flashes
quick-minted from the light across the tomb.
And as it spins
the air's eyes seem to stare,
the shrine hushed waiting,
as if the saint's hand
were hovering ready,
cupped to catch your name
before the spinning ends.

SIMON BAILEY

Intercessor

Angry prayers come from the heart
so let us be angry.
Cursing and swearing,
bellowing our profanities let us summon the angels.

When angry, cut to the heart
furiously bleeding we are quickened to action
tear the flesh, the sleek flesh
that hides our famine from the hungry.

White knuckle. Red knuckle.
Torn by our hammering
on the barred door
closed on our hearts.

Minds racing
as lifebloods draining uncupped.
Emptying us out on the street
dripping, drips no longer. Done.

Too late.

Too late the angels
gather us lifeless
in through the portal.

But we were heard in those moments.
Heard at our shrillest
and moved to action.
All are gathered in.

JONATHAN FORD

Retreat

The strong may seek
their scallop shell of quiet
in voluntary isolation,
to replenish
what the turmoil of the world
has drained away.

What of the weak,
whose solitary hermit shell
is like a prison,
permanent, unchosen,
— to whom the world
has never given?

JOAN ROWBOTTOM

Friends' Meeting

very nearly a non-swimmer
I have just enough breaststroke
to save my soul.

Sundays, I take deep breaths
and go in to test my strength.

debris of house and home
bump and bruise
my outstretched hands;

tangles of the week and work
loop round my legs
to lure me down;

but often, amazed,
I achieve my width;
buoyed up, it seems,
by the quiet strokes
of others, friends,
mutually striving
to stay afloat,

and aiming in the
same direction.

NADINE VOKINS

To a Lady Saying Grace in a Station Buffet

Step nearer to my canvas gracious traveller
That I may paint a portrait of you
Sitting tranquilly against a backcloth
Of trains and timetables,
As, mindful of Cana, you offer thanks
For lukewarm coffee
And the veiled hostility of slab cake.

SHEILA NOTTAGE

Members One of Another

I was seeing with my inward eye the other day,
peering out through my mouth
and looking at the backs of my teeth.
I could feel the hair growing on my head
and on my lip
(like Heimdall hearing the wool growing on the sheep's backs).
My breath leapt over my hot tongue
and joined with the outside air
as a river with the sea,
merging my living body
into the outside world.
My aura of body heat was doing the same
less consciously.

I am continuous with the world beyond me,
mixing invisibly and inextricably with it,
and it with me, its random particles and radiations,
its heat and sounds,
penetrating my thin skin, unknowing.
A kiss, a hand-clasp, is an interchange of auras.
We are members one of another,
closer than hand or eye.
Not so much reaction as our way of life.
Let us not to the marriage of our lives,
the concord of our minds,
admit impediment.
O world indivisible, we know you,
with or without the silence
of the inward eye.

ERIC WOOD
First published in *The Friends' Quarterly*

Bleak Day

When your day
is a cube of despair —
lead casket boxing in
your soul to straitened time
and space — and where
you feel contracted fatally
to nothingness — don't air
(Pandora-lavish) that barbed swarm,
grievances non-retractable —
to sting, to curse the world!

Kneel down, shoot sheer a prayer
(past low doubt's ceiling,
through the fragile hatch
of possibility)
that He will come —
He whom death's dungeon walls
and barred doors can't deter.

See! With His key
of golden-wrought surprise
He's instant there!
Your bleak day's now
a stage set for His company
and His grace
to act on.
      Hear Him swear
'Lo . . . I am with you always
ALL your days!'

GRACE WESTERDUIN

Orison

God, tha knaws I'm nut one to mek a fuss,
onnly ther's no point i' wastin' mi breath —
Luther spoke o' Deus absconditus
an' nah others is on abaht thi death.
Ther's nooan mich sense i' my natterin' on,
troublin' deaf 'eaven, a sheer bloomin' void;
if it's a case o' talkin' to missen
I need mi 'ead seen to — an' that theer Freud
said it all comes fro' summat deep inside,
super-ego an' id, atavastic fear,
subjective feelin's 'at can't be denied,
no transcendent other at all out theer.
But if ther's nowt an' nobody beyond,
why does summat in me want to respond?

KENNETH WADSWORTH

Disclosure

Prayer is like watching for the
Kingfisher. All you can do is
Be where he is likely to appear, and
Wait.
Often, nothing much happens;
There is space, silence and
Expectancy.
No visible sign, only the
Knowledge that he's been there
And may come again.
Seeing or not seeing cease to matter,
You have been prepared.
But when you've almost stopped
Expecting it, a flash of brightness
Gives encouragement.

ANN LEWIN

Hospital Rosary

Silly honourable thing,
Clover among the roses
Solid earthy beads —
The stepping stones
Bridging my distress
Linking our pain to His,
Restoring peace through their smoothness
Blending my life
In all its fragmentation —
In the rhythm of repetition —
To His infinite wholeness.
Unpretentious occupation,
His to work
And mine to be.
The movement of my hands
And the flow of ancient prayers
Praying me.

AMY PURDON

Bread and Wine

The Chalice

My God! The singing was in tune! It
Lifted from us. As from a choir of
Earthly angels. We stood singing
Shoulder to shoulder, hand to hand
Eye to laughing eye and heart
To heart. The circle of our
Standing was completed by
The altar; an altar with
A chalice waiting while
We sang and said the
Usual things but now
Transformed.   It
Waited, shining
While our
Kiss of
Peace
Bubbled with
Affectionate
Embraces.
Waited
For the silence
That would come
Which   always
Comes   upon
The breaking
Of the
Bread
And when
We took it
Lo! the wine was
Christ! All wine, all
Joy, all love, poured into
Our brimming lives. And when we
Sang again, it was in tune with You
AND   WE   SANG   ALLELUIA!

THELMA FISHER
First published in *Christian*

Bread and Wine

Like you,
Says Jesus,
I am divine;
As a bottle
Filled with wine.

Like you,
I am bread;
Just as human,
Just as crumbly,
So he said.

You, like me,
(The words were spoken),
Were born to be broken,
Crumbled and shed,
That Love's volume
May be read.

ERNEST CHITTY

The Supper

And did you mean this when
cheek by jowl with companions, your
hands on the shared table broke
bread and passed wine with words
which held heart, checked breath
as only joy or fear can; this
my body, my blood?

Did you mean us, crouched
in the posture of repentance, with-
drawn from each other, locked
in Sunday's formal mummery with
God aloof in sanctuary where
few seek shelter; this
your body, your blood?

SIMON IREDALE

Crossbred

The Bread was rough
And brownly stable-baked
In fiercest heat
In dry, brown hay sown
Without rich yeast
To help it rise

We make it soft
And white
Cutting away the darker crust
That had no form
Or beauty
Of its own

We bake it soft
And barely feel it break
Beneath our hands.

The wood was coarse
And redly moistened by the curse
Of generations
Splintered by our hate
Our father's sins
And our children's indifference

We smooth and polish
To obliterate
The coarse-grained
Love-worn face
To see only the image
Of ourselves.

Afraid of truth
We try to sandpaper
The way to life.

IAIN D. CUNNINGHAM

I love the sunshine in the kitchen,
The glory of the light awakens
All the familiar textures of pot and china.
This is the home of the house,
The centre of its warmth,
The articulation of its love,
In the rise of bread, the crust of pie,
And the richness of gravy.
It is the place of your caring,
Fleshed out in the daily details,
Too small to be noted one by one,
But each constructing the heart of the house.

Your delight in us is incarnated here,
And this is the place of our true receiving.
Here we came hungry, thirsty and in our need,
To meet the kindness of your hands.
And your friends came,
Finding a warmth they sought and a love they craved.
Not a pretentious place,
A good cause or a moral crusade.
If you will, another Nazareth,
Hidden in the wilderness of the world,
Where kindness feeds a poor Christ and his friends,
And bids them come in from the dark.

TIM MARKS

Eucharist ...

The chalice slipped.
The wine that was not
Just wine spilled
The blood of Christ
In front of the altar.
And through the tension
That like a cloud of incense
Enveloped the watchers
Glowed the truth that we shared.
Our communion heightened
By the closeness of that blood
Shed in the dust of then
For our salvation now
We kneeled in awe
Before the stain of love.

CHRISTINE M. McINTOSH

Body Gift

He spent hours in days and years
keeping her company,
in talk and silence, doing things and nothing,
touching to certain limits,
hunger aroused and half assuaged,
in constant, half unconscious hope
of knowing of her mystery,
in her and on her,
united to a physical limit
as instinct in flesh would have it be.
Wanting that body, the sacrament of her presence;
in giving, would give her all,
and thus enflesh him
in the body of the race that
from a beginning procreated life,
for now and the life time of this time.

She spent hours in days and years
keeping Him company,
in prayer and silence, working, resting,
touched in the secret parts of her spirit,
hunger aroused, never to be assuaged
in constant and articulate hope
of being known in His infinite mystery.
This Body given to her, in her,
drinking His life Blood,
as instinct of spirit would have it be.
Thus joined to a body of people
sharing one god-life,
lovingly procreating believers' love-life,
for now and the all-time that is no-time.

Clumsy Ritual

Emergency priest,
call to intensive care.
A man drowning in air,
failing heart, desperate eyes.
Wife close with constant caressing,
cajoling, encouraging, with power of
woman, lover, mother, nurse,
holding her man to this life.

the sacrament given hurriedly, clumsily,
amid scrabbling for mask,
oxygen, healing drug.
Prayers like an empty last shout.
Son, facing his father's going,
turned away at religion's empty effort.

But not so.
Next day, the man twenty years younger,
care, drugs and prayer had worked.
And his wife still there
with endless healing touch of love.

GERARD BURNS

Acknowledgements

With thanks to the following publishers:

Canon Books
    Landscapes of the Heart by Geoffrey Smith
Dedalus Press
    Road, with Cypress and Star by John F. Deane, 1988
Freedom Press
    The Excitement Of Being Sam by James Russell Grant
Goldsmith Press
    Collected Poems by Desmond Egan
Hale and Iremonger
    Passengers to the City by Katherine Gallagher, 1985
Headland Publications
    "A Question of Wood" by Peggy Poole
Lazerwolf Books
    Rage Without Anger by Bill Lewis, 1988
Mandeville Press
    The Single Mind by Sybil Birch, 1980
Mayhew-McCrimmon
    Begotten in Silence by Kevin Nichols, 1978
Outposts Publications
    Beautiful Man, by Alwyn Marriage, 1977
Stride
    Dandelions for Mothers' Day by Angela Topping, 1988
    Leasing

Magazines and Journals

Brixton Mortar
Christian
Encounter
Envoi 80
The Friends' Quarterly
New Fire
Poetry Wales
Prospice

Index of Poets